Constitution: Fact or Fiction

Constitution: Fact or Fiction

is available for $14.95 from either Dr. Schroder or Buffalo Creek Press at the addresses below.
Quantity discounts are available.

Colorado residents add 3% sales tax if ordering from Colorado;
Texas residents add 7.25% sales tax if ordering from Texas.

Other Books and Videos by Dr. Eugene Schroder

War and Emergency Powers - Video
War and Emergency Powers - Special Report and Supporting Documents

Available from **Dr. Eugene Schroder**
PO Box 89
Campo, CO 81029

For information, call 719 -787-9958

Other Books by Micki Nellis

Makin' It on the Farm:
Alcohol Fuel is the Road to Independence
How to make fuel alcohol in small plants

Logan and the Duck Patrol
First of a series of children's picture books designed to teach moral values and build self-esteem

Available from **Buffalo Creek Press**
PO Box 2424, Cleburne, TX 76031
Voice 817-641-4908, 800-610-4908
FAX 817-641-0901

Constitution: Fact or Fiction

The Story of the Nation's Descent
from a Constitutional Republic
through a Constitutional Dictatorship
to an Unconstitutional Dictatorship

Dr. Eugene Schroder

with Micki Nellis

Buffalo Creek Press
Cleburne, Texas

Buffalo Creek Press
603 N. Main Street
Cleburne, TX 76031

Library Cataloging Aid by Buffalo Creek Press

Schroder, Eugene
Constitution: Fact or Fiction / Eugene Schroder, with Micki Nellis
Includes index.
Includes bibliography.
Includes glossary.
ISBN 1-885534-06-X : $14.95
Library of Congress Catalog Card Number 94-79634
1. Current Affairs. 2. Social Science. 3. Constitutional Law.
4. History. I. Nellis, Micki. II. Title.

Published 1995, First Edition

20 19 18 17 1615 14 13 12 11 10 9 8 7 6 5 4 3 2
Printed in the United States of America

Dedication

to Laurie Schroder

wife, mother, friend and fighter
in gratitude and appreciation

Acknowledgements

to
Ed Petrowsky
Russell Grider
Alvin Jenkins
Van Stafford
and Derral Schroder

without whose help and research
this effort would not have been possible

Table of Contents

1	Our Constitution Has Been Suspended	1
2	What the Government Can Do When the Constitution is Suspended	5
3	Why the Revolutionary War Was Fought	11
4	Rights the Constitution Guaranteed Us	15
5	What We Have Lost	21
6	Money, Property, Production Were Nationalized	25
7	Entrenchment of War Powers	87
8	War Powers in Germany, France and England	113
9	States Rights Feud Becomes War	119
10	Military Rule Over Civilians	125
11	War Powers From 1913 to 1932	135
12	Emergencies Proliferate Under Recent Presidents	141
13	War Money and Peace Money	165
14	Healing the Nation	177
	Appendix A - What Can I Do?	179
	Appendix B - Declaration of Independence	189
	Appendix C - Constitution of the United States	195
	Glossary	221
	Bibliography	233
	Index	237

Chapter One

Our Constitution Has Been Suspended

Since March 9, 1933, the United States has been in a state of declared National Emergency.

-Senate Report 93-549

When in the course of human events, ordinary citizens have reason to fear their government, it's time to look seriously at cause and cure.

Government officials are supposed to be instruments by which we, the people, govern ourselves. Under a constitutional government, the citizens are the ruling class. All other offices are subservient to the citizens. How did citizens become the subjects of government and government officials become the ruling class?

Government Has Achieved Ability to Rule by Decree

The US Constitution was basically the shackles placed on the federal government by a sovereign people. The people possessed God-given rights. These rights were only *secured* by the constitution. All rights not specifically granted to the government were reserved for the people.

This country started out as a constitutional republic, that is, a union of sovereign nation states. The federal government was to be an agent of the states.

As a safeguard, the constitution provides that during times of rebellion or invasion, the president may assume all powers. These emergency powers should end after the crisis. President Lincoln assumed all powers during the Civil War. Since he was dealing with a rebellion, we may say that he established a constitutional dictatorship.

Since then, however, the definition of "emergencies" requiring total control has been stretched to include economic problems, social imbalances, and perceived threats to the US by a foreign country's actions on another continent. When authoritarian control is exerted during times other than rebellion or enemy invasion, it is an unconstitutional dictatorship. The federal government has overstepped the bounds placed on it by the constitution.

Through the insidious, yet steady encroachment of "emergency powers," the government has now achieved the ability to rule the people by statute or decree, without the vote or consent of the ruled. Through a maze of political maneuvers, the emergency powers granted to President Franklin D. Roosevelt in 1933 to deal with an economic depression have become part of the US Code as permanent everyday powers. America has continued under the "unconstitutional dictatorship" of war and emergency powers to this day, more than 60 years later.

Emergency Rule Means Government Owns All Rights

In reality, under this "unconstitutional dictatorship," the roles have been reversed. We have no rights except those the government grants us. Under our constitutional government, we the people had all rights except those specifically granted to the government.

We have lost our constitutional rights. How did it happen? What does it mean? What can we do about it? Increasingly, US citizens are unwilling to be the pawns of arbitrary and capricious decrees. We have both the right and duty to reclaim our country.

The government today, with its inflated bureaucracy, political posturing, and ineffectual programs, would be a laughingstock if it weren't for the sinister side - arbitrary seizure of property without proven cause by many government agencies, federally mandated but unfunded programs that choke the states' right to rule themselves, an unsound money system, and a de facto economic depression for the last 10 years. Add a growing separation between "haves" and "have nots" and we have a powder keg on a short fuse.

Government has grown so big, so unreachable, that the ordinary citizen feels helpless to influence it. Government by the people? Even those with clout and political savvy, such as state governors, seem unable to sway D.C.

Government acts like a tyrant gone rampant, wilfully imposing its policies on citizens, protecting its image, and covering up its mistakes. Fear sets in when we realize that the government can play kickball with our lives - and there is no one to stop it. Today, with our constitutional rights effectively suspended, we are at the mercy of the giant.

Hitler used Germany's emergency powers clause (Article 48) to perpetrate his atrocities. Granted, no US president has even approached Hitler's dictatorship, but he has the power to do so. The difference is the degree of benevolence with which the US government has ruled and with which Hitler ruled.

The US constitution provides for the president to be granted emergency powers in times of war or enemy attack. The fatal flaw in the constitution, however, is that once the president has these powers, he himself must give them up. Eleven presidents, both Democrat and Republican, have failed to reinstate the constitution and give up these emergency powers. Today we see the president and entrenched bureaucracy passing rules through the executive branch's many agencies without challenge from the other two branches of government - the congress and the judiciary.

We Have Been Under Emergency Rule for 61 Years

Senate Report 93-549, written in 1973, said "Since March 9, 1933, the United States has been in a state of declared national emergency." It goes on to say:

"A majority of the people of the United States have lived all their lives under emergency rule. For 40 years, freedoms and governmental procedures guaranteed by the constitution have, in varying degrees, been abridged by laws brought into force by states of National emergency. In the United States, actions taken by government in times of great crisis have... in important ways shaped the present phenomenon of a permanent state of National emergency."...

"These proclamations give force to 470 provisions of federal law. These hundreds of statutes delegate to the President extraordinary powers, ordinarily exercised by Congress, which affect the lives of American citizens in a host of all-encompassing manners. This vast range of powers, taken together, confer enough authority to rule this country without reference to normal constitutional process.

"Under the powers delegated by these statutes, the President may: seize property, organize and control the means of production; seize commodities; assign military forces abroad; institute martial law; seize and control all transportation and communication; regulate the operation of private enterprise; restrict travel; and, in a plethora of particular ways, control the lives of all American citizens."

Today most of the people living in the US have not been taught the constitution, have never enjoyed the constitutional rights for which our forefathers fought a revolutionary war, and know that something is terribly wrong with our government yet have no idea what to do about it.

Knowledge is power. Once the American people understand what has happened, they will demand just and reasonable action. It was said of the Revolutionary War against Great Britain in 1776 that the real revolution occurred in the hearts and minds of the American people before a shot was fired.

God grant that we may have a revolution in the hearts and minds of the American people without a shot being fired.

Chapter Two

What the Government Can Do When the Constitution is Suspended

It is not the function of the government to keep the citizen from falling into error; it is the function of the citizen to keep the government from falling into error.

-US Supreme Court

Good People Get into Trouble

You probably think that if you lead a straight life and obey the rules, you aren't going to get into trouble, right? Wrong. Consider these examples:

Diane, a soft-spoken school teacher, was called to serve on the grand jury. She was asked to fill out a lengthy form disclosing everything about herself, including how much money she made, how much her house was worth, what kind of car she drove, etc. She would not answer the questions because she thought this was an invasion of privacy and she didn't see how it affected her right to serve on a jury. The judge had her arrested for contempt of court and jailed.

Linda, a young mother, was getting ready to go to work one morning when a Child Protective Service worker showed up on her doorstep. She insisted on coming in, inspecting the house and four-year-old Johnny, and looking for signs of child abuse. Linda showed up at work in tears two hours later, but it wasn't over. She received a call at work asking both her and her husband to come in for an interview. More grilling. Files were made on the parents. The young couple had to supply references, and the child protective service worker called these people asking if they had seen any signs of child abuse. The visits and interviews continued for six months. The reason for all this? Someone called in a "tip." The agency refused to tell the young couple who called, but it didn't take them long to figure out it was a former friend who held a grudge.

Janette and Bob were selling a house and buying another one. In the packet of forms for the closing was a report that a woman with the same first and last names, but a different middle name and a different social security number, had declared bankruptcy six years previously. Janette had to prove that she wasn't that person, including getting forms notarized, which required going to three different bureaucracies. Janette's realtor told her that since November, 1993, buyers' names are run through a computer, which sometimes comes up with 25 or so similar names. The buyer has to prove he is none of those people.

Don got a notice in the mail from his bank that his account had been attached by the IRS. No notice, no warning, no reason, no appeal.

Bob owned a piece of land some distance from his home. When he visited it, he found that it had been confiscated by the government because they had found illegal drug activity on it. He had to prove he was not involved and had no knowledge of it before he could have his land back.

Government Agents May Knock Down Our Doors

A crippled old black man was in bed asleep one night when a drug squad burst in and sprayed him with bullets. They claimed he was resisting arrest. The squad had a tip that a young man who sometimes visited the elderly gentleman was into drugs, but the young man didn't live there and in fact, wasn't there that night. The slain man's son, a well-known sports figure, demonstrated on TV how crippled his father was and how he would have had to go through a series of slow and painful maneuvers to even sit up on the side of the bed.

The Bureau of Alcohol, Tobacco and Firearms fiasco in Waco, Texas was played out on national TV. What isn't widely known is that the original warrants were for a total of $400 for two guns suspected of not having had the excise tax paid on them. This justified attacking a private residence with a riot squad, laying siege to the compound for two months at a cost of over a million dollars a day to taxpayers, imprisoning and torturing men, women and children for over two months without benefit of charges being filed or a trial being held, and in the end the deaths of 86 people plus four ATF troopers. Incidentally, the survivors were acquitted by a jury of charges of conspiracy to commit murder.

Senseless Rules Waste Our Time

A young couple wanted to pull their trailer from Virginia to Texas, but the trailer was unlicensed. He called his mom in Texas to buy him a trailer license. Mom called the licensing office in the county in which the son lived and told them what she needed, inquired about their hours and explained that she was 60 miles away. When she arrived, they refused to issue a license on the trailer because she did not have proof that the car which would pull the trailer had insurance. Her explanations that the car was in Virginia fell on deaf ears. So too did her question as to why they didn't tell her that before she drove 120 miles round trip. She went back home and called the local county agency and they told her just to bring in any proof of insurance on any car. Makes a lot of sense, doesn't it?

Guilty Until We Prove Ourselves Innocent

If you are found with more than $10,000 cash on your person, it can be confiscated. You must prove how you earned it and that it is legally yours.

If you deposit or withdraw $10,000 or more from your bank account, the bank is required by law to report it to the IRS.

If you get in trouble with one agency, another agency often investigates you (usually the IRS).

These are just a few everyday examples of real people and their small and large troubles with government agencies.

Examples Are Common in Everyday Life

These situations are so common that you can easily find other examples in the problems of your family and friends.

Some Acts Are Inherently Wrong; Others Are Just Against the Rules

We are not saying there should be no punishment for crimes. Some acts are inherently wrong - murder, rape, kidnapping, arson, etc. But some acts are "crimes" only because some legislative body or bureaucrat has made a law that says it is. Another agency may even have a conflicting rule. These "crimes" change regularly depending on who is in power. Legal terminology makes the distinction between *malum se* - evil in itself, versus *malum prohibitum* - a crime because someone has made a law against it.

The story of Daniel in the Bible illustrates this point. Daniel was accustomed to praying every day from his window. The ruler made it against the law for anyone to pray. Daniel continued to do so. He was seized and thrown into the lion's den because he broke the law.

In our case, our liberties have been taken from us and are being sold back to us in the form of licenses.

A person doesn't stop knowing how to drive if he misplaces his drivers license. A merchant doesn't lose his ability to run a business if he has no commercial license. A farmer doesn't stop being a steward of the land if he doesn't get a pesticide applicator's license.

Restricted Liberties Have Not Bought Safety

Even though many of our liberties have been taken, the system still isn't working. The streets are not safe, drugs and violence are rampant in schools, young couples can't make a living for their families, many elderly are starving and neglected, and millions of Americans can't afford health care. Restricted liberty did not buy us safety and well-being.

What Can't the Government Do to Us?

What can government agencies do to us if they suspect us of not following their arbitrary edicts that may change tomorrow? Anything they wish. They can and do:

Rob our time and productivity with senseless rules and paperwork.
Invade our privacy.
Take our money and property.
Throw us in jail.
Take our children from us.
Ruin our reputation.
Kill us.

We Have No Recourse

Do we have any recourse? Not really. Most people don't have the time and money to fight.

Our only hope is big media attention and public outcry. Few have the ear of the media. We are alone when we are pitted against the various government agencies with their awesome and arbitrary power.

Chapter Three

Why the Revolutionary War Was Fought

Since the close of the last war, the British Parliament, claiming the power of right to bind the people of America by statute in all cases whatsoever ...

- Declaration of Rights, 1774

England Looked on Colonies as Property

The colonists were in a new land fending for themselves. They either learned self-reliance and responsibility or they didn't survive.

England gave them no help to speak of. To England, America was a group of trading companies whose purpose was to further Great Britain's dominion over the world. King George regarded England as the owner of the colonies and the colonists, and used them to enrich the Crown.

Colonies Had No Sound Money System

The colonies had no official money. They were greatly hampered in trade by the many different types of trade "coin." They used furs, tobacco, wampum (mussel shells made into beads), French louis, English guineas, German thalers, Dutch ducats, Spanish doubloons, and the Spanish milled dollar, or piece of eight.

England ignored the needs of the colonies and made no effort to provide gold or silver coin or small change currency.

The Massachusetts Bay Company started minting coins in Boston in 1652. Other colonies and individuals tried minting projects but generally failed. The new land still did not have a standard money.

England Levies Taxes on Colonists to Finance War

The British got into a war with Spain. They needed more and more wealth to pay for it. They took more and more from the colonies.

The British levied taxes on tea and tobacco and stamps to raise money for the war. They made arbitrary rules and expected the colonists to obey. The rules could change at any time.

The colonists began to complain of "taxation without representation."

England Uses Force

The British tightened the rules. They put on shows of force. They attacked villagers, burned towns, and plundered the coasts and seas. The final blow was when the colonists learned large numbers of foreign mercenaries were sailing toward the new world in order to subdue the colonists.

Colonists Declare Independence

Representatives of the people met in Philadelphia in 1776 to decide what to do. After long and bitter debate and soul searching, these men asked Thomas Jefferson to draft the Declaration of Independence to tell the world why the colonists were cutting their ties with Great Britain.

Let's look at some excerpts.The second paragraph says:

"We hold these truths to be self-evident, that all men are created equal; that they are endowed by their Creator with certain unalienable rights; that among these are life, liberty, and the pursuit of happiness. That to secure these rights, governments are instituted among men, deriving their just powers from the consent of the governed; that whenever any form of government becomes destructive of these ends, it is the right of the people to alter or to abolish it, and to institute new government, laying its foundation on such principles, and organizing its powers in such form, as to them shall seem most likely to effect their safety and happiness..."

It goes on to say this step is not taken lightly, that the colonists have been very patient.

Complaints Against King George

It begins to set forth the complaints against King George. Several complaints deal with his refusal to make fair laws, to make needed laws, to allow representation by the colonists, and his dissolving bodies of representatives repeatedly when they disagreed with him.

Then we come to these complaints:

"He has made judges dependent on his will alone, for the tenure of their offices, and the amount and payment of their salaries.

"He has erected a multitude of new offices, and sent hither swarms of officers to harass our people, and to eat out their substance.

"He has kept among us, in times of peace, standing armies, without the consent of our legislatures.

"He has affected to render the military independent of, and superior to, the civil power.

"He has combined with others to subject us to a jurisdiction foreign to our Constitution, and unacknowledged by our laws, giving his assent to their acts of pretended legislation.

"For quartering large bodies of armed troops among us:..."

We have some of these situations today.

The ending words:

"And for the support of this declaration, with a firm reliance on the protection of Divine Providence, we mutually pledge to each other our lives, our fortune, and our sacred honor."

With the signing came seven long years of bloodshed and destruction.

Chapter Four

Rights the Constitution Guaranteed Us

The powers not delegated to the United States by the constitution, nor prohibited by it to the states, are reserved to the states respectively, or to the people.
- United States Constitution

When the colonists declared themselves independent, they had already begun to think of themselves as a new people, as Americans.

After they defeated the British, they were determined never again to be the subjects of tyrants and despotism, either from without or within.

They began to hammer out the philosophy of the United States.

First they formed into a loose confederation of states. One problem was that the individual states could easily ignore the confederation, and there was nothing to prevent one state declaring war on another, as was common in Europe.

States Rights Versus Federal Supremacy

Out of this grew a great debate between the Federalists and the Anti Federalists.

The Federalists felt that a stronger union was needed to ensure domestic peace, represent the new country abroad, protect the country, and strengthen the growing nation.

The Anti Federalists feared a strong central government would put them back into a situation like the one they had fought to overthrow for seven years.

Eventually a consensus was reached. The Constitution of the United States was drafted. Its great purpose was to preserve peace on this continent and ensure liberty. Americans became citizens of both their states and the new nation. Because of this dual citizenship, the American Constitution formed a federal republic.

(It was a republic because not everyone could vote. Only free white males could vote. The country did not become a democracy until the constitution was amended to allow everyone the right to vote, including African-Americans, Indians, and women.)

Coming out of oppression and despotism, the founding fathers tried to craft a constitution that would ensure equality, opportunity and justice for all, for all time.

They spelled out the rights of the people and said that all rights not specifically given to the federal government or the states were reserved for the people.

Human Beings Have Inalienable Rights

The Constitution clearly stated that all human beings have certain inalienable rights just because they belong to the human species. Among these inalienable human rights are the right to life, liberty, and the pursuit of happiness. The Constitution sought to form a government with the consent of the governed, one that would ensure domestic tranquillity, a common national defense, and promote the general welfare and secure the blessings of liberty for everyone.

Individual rights were reinforced with the "bill of rights" (the first ten amendments), and other amendments later on.

(The complete Constitution may be found in the Appendix.)

Let‘s look at the rights guaranteed by the Constitution. At the same time, let's think about whether these rights are real for us today, or whether they exist on paper only.

Article One - Freedom of Speech, Religion, Press

Congress shall make no law respecting the establishment of religion, or prohibiting the free exercise thereof, or abridging the freedom of speech, or of the press; or of the right of the people peaceably to assemble, and to petition the Government for a redress of grievances.

Article Two - Right to Bear Arms

A well-regulated militia being necessary to the security of a free state, the right of the people to keep and bear arms shall not be infringed.

Article Three - No Soldiers Quartered in Peacetime

No soldier shall, in time of peace, be quartered in any house, without the consent of the owner, nor in time of war but in a manner to be prescribed by law.

Article Four- No Unlawful Search and Seizure

The right of the people to be secure in their persons, houses, papers, and effects, against unreasonable searches and seizures, shall not be violated, and no warrants shall issue, but upon probable cause, supported by oath or affirmation, and particularly describing the place to be searched, and the persons or things to be seized.

Article Five - Grand Jury Indictment Required

No person shall be held to answer for a capital, or otherwise infamous crime, unless on a presentment or indictment of a grand jury, except in cases arising in the land or naval forces, or in the militia, when in actual service in time of war or public danger; nor shall any person be subject for the same offense to be twice put in jeopardy of life or limb; nor shall be compelled in any criminal case to be a witness against himself, nor be deprived of life, liberty, or property, without due process of law; nor shall private property be taken for public use, without just compensation.

Article Six - Right to Speedy Trial

In all criminal prosecutions the accused shall enjoy the right to a speedy and public trial, by an impartial jury of the state and district wherein the crime shall have been committed, which district shall have been previously ascertained by law, and to be informed of the nature and cause of the accusation; to be confronted with the witnesses against him; to have compulsory process for obtaining witnesses in his favor, and to have the assistance of counsel for his defense.

Article Seven - Right to Trial by Jury

In suits at common law, where the value in controversy shall exceed twenty dollars, the right of trial by jury shall be preserved, and no fact tried by a jury shall be otherwise re-examined in any court of the United States, than according to the rules of common law.

Article Eight - No Excessive Bail or Punishment

Excessive bail shall not be required, nor excessive fines imposed, nor cruel and unusual punishments be inflicted.

Article Nine - People Retain Rights Not Assigned

The enumeration in the Constitution of certain rights shall not be construed to deny or disparage others retained by the people.

Article Ten - All Other Rights Go to State or People

The powers not delegated to the United States by the Constitution, nor prohibited by it to the states, are reserved to the states respectively, or to the people.

Other Rights Assured the People

In addition, slavery was abolished by Article 13. Article 14 made citizens of all persons born or naturalized in the United States and forbade any state to abridge the privileges and immunities of citizenship.

The 15th Amendment said the right to vote shall not be denied by the United States or any state on account of race, color, or previous condition of servitude.

The 24th outlawed poll taxes. The 19th Amendment gave women the right to vote. The 26th Amendment lowered the voting age to 18.

With this collection of amendments, the right to vote was finally given to all adults.

Thus the founding fathers laid out our rights clearly and plainly in common language after much debate and soul-searching.

Chapter Five

What We Have Lost

A majority of the people of the United States have lived all their lives under emergency rule.

- Senate Report 93-549

We Have Lost Our Constitutional Rights

Today we are presumed guilty until we prove ourselves innocent.Today we have Big Brother watching us, invading our privacy, gathering information and controlling our lives. We have all but lost our right to keep and bear arms.

We are not secure in our persons, houses, papers and effects against unreasonable searches and seizures. We are subjected to electronic snooping, wiretapping, and drug raiders kicking down our door at any time. Wrong door? Sorry.

We are subject to confiscation of property and bank accounts at any time by various government agencies.

We are subject to Child Protective Services invading our homes to make us prove we don't abuse our children.

We are held to answer for "crimes" without benefit of charges being filed or a trial being held.

The news is full of people being tried twice for the same crime, in criminal court and in civil court, or on criminal charges, then on federal charges.

We do not enjoy speedy trials. Several years may lapse before a case is tried.

We are not allowed trial by jury in civil cases unless we file a petition and pay for it in advance. Most civil cases are not heard by juries.

Bail and fines are excessive if the accused has no hopes of meeting them, and that is often the case. The amount of time and money it takes to appeal a government agency confiscation or ruling is prohibitive to the common working man or woman.

Cruel and unusual punishment? The world saw what happened at Waco. Texas. This was cruel and unusual punishment without benefit of charges, trial or conviction.

The Constitution says all legislative powers herein granted shall be vested in the congress. Where does it mention the Federal Register, a device by which a proposed law can be published by a government agency or bureaucracy, a certain time allowed for public comment, and then the law cemented without regard for what the comment was? Hundreds of proposed rules and regulations are published here each week. Most people have never heard of the Federal Register.

The president can also make law by executive orders and proclamations.

Congress was given the power to coin money and to regulate the value thereof. So why does the Federal Reserve do this today?

Congress was given the power to declare war. So why does the president order invasions without counsel of the congress?

Congress was given the right to call forth the militia to suppress insurrections and repel invasions. So why does the president declare martial law and use federal troops inside the US? Why does the president maintain a standing army among us?

The Constitution says "No capitation or other direct tax shall be laid, unless in proportion to the census or enumeration herein before directed to be taken." The amendment establishing the income tax was passed when few congressmen were present, and many say illegally.

The Constitution says "The privilege of the writ of habeas corpus shall not be suspended, unless in cases of invasion or rebellion the public safety may require it." This means that a person should be brought before the court and charged with the alleged crime. This clause means it is illegal to hold someone without charging them with a crime.

"No bill of attainder or *ex post facto* law shall be passed." What do you call a retroactive income tax regulation?

"No state shall make anything but gold and silver coin a tender in payment of debts ..." So why was gold coin illegal for many years? Why aren't Federal Reserve bank notes backed by gold or silver?

Under the duties of the judicial branch, Article Three, it says "The trial of all crimes, except in cases of impeachment, shall be by jury;..." So why are we not automatically given a trial by jury?

The constitution says the people shall have the right to keep and bear arms. Now laws are being passed to abridge that right.

Article Six says "The Constitution and the laws of the United States which shall be made in pursuance thereof ... shall be the supreme law of the land; and the judges in every state shall be bound thereby ...". So why can we not use the constitution in court as defense against violation of our rights?

The answer to all these questions is that the federal government has used and abused the constitution's war and emergency powers clause so that for over 60 years our constitution has been suspended.

Chapter Six

Money, Property and Production Were Nationalized

Under these powers the president may: seize property; organize and control the means of production; seize commodities; assign military forces abroad; institute martial law; seize and control all transportation and communication; regulate the operation of private enterprise; restrict travel, and in a plethora of particular ways, control the lives of all American citizens. - *Senate Report 93-549*

President Franklin D. Roosevelt responded to the great economic depression in 1933 by using war and emergency powers intended only for dealing with rebellion or enemy invasion.

During his first 100 days in office, he seized all gold and silver, took the country off the gold standard and established a banking system based on the debts of the people, expanded the Trading With the Enemy Act to redefine "enemy" as including all the American people, established government control over natural resources, the social agenda and welfare, utilities, private financing, industry, labor and transportation, and bailed out the banks. Roosevelt's acts abrogated the gold clause in all public and private contracts, thus usurping the legality of private contracts. At the same time he established control over financing and the price of homes, and inserted into the Agricultural Adjustment Act a clause which shifted the power to coin money and regulate its value (granted by the constitution to congress) from congress to the president.

In addition, the government decreed that ownership of all property is in the State, that individual ownership is only by virtue of the government, amounting to mere user, and that use must be in accordance with the law and subordinate to the necessities of the state.

Time Travel - Dateline America, 1933

On October 24, 1929, the stock market crashed.

Breadlines appeared.

Shacks made of packing boxes, scrap iron, and materials picked out of dumps sprang up on the outskirts of towns in settlements called "Hoovervilles."

Whole families slept on automobile seats pillaged from wrecking yards and warmed themselves before fires of rubbish in grease drums.

Homeless people slept in doorways and on park benches, begging from restaurants half-eaten biscuits and pie crusts to keep themselves alive.

Hitchhikers thumbed rides on the highways hoping to get to someplace better. Transients rode the freight cars. Hoboes begged food and shelter.

The great depression had begun.

By the time President Franklin D. Roosevelt took office on March 4, 1933, people were lining up at banks to withdraw their deposits of gold.

In his inaugural address, Roosevelt said he would not hesitate to call for "broad Executive power to wage a war against the emergency, as great as the power that would be given to me if we were in fact invaded by a foreign foe."

He was talking about war and emergency powers, which the constitution provided for in case of rebellion or enemy invasion if the public safety required it.

This was neither a rebellion or enemy invasion.

The next day, March 5, President Roosevelt issued Proclamation 2038 calling a special session of the congress to convene March 9, 1933.

One day later, on March 6, he called a governors conference and persuaded them to pass a resolution pledging support for giving him emergency war powers.

That same day, March 6, he proclaimed a bank holiday extending from Monday, March 6 through Thursday, March

9 (Proclamation 2039). The order stopped withdrawals of gold from the banks by the owners of that gold, the same people who had deposited that gold in the first place, on penalty of a fine of not more than $10,000 and/or ten years in jail.

On March 8, the Federal Reserve Board asked the banks to prepare a list of people who had recently withdrawn gold or gold certificates and who had not re-deposited them by March 13 (the date was later extended.) It was announced that the list of names would be published.

On March 9, President Roosevelt issued Proclamation 2040 saying that the emergency still existed, and it was necessary to take further measures extending beyond March 9, 1933, therefore all the provisions of Proclamation 2039 of March 6 "are hereby continued in full force and effect until further proclamation by the President."

The evening of March 9, at 8:30 p.m., the congress passed an act that approved and confirmed the president's actions and the Secretary of Treasury's actions since March 4th. It also gave the Secretary of the Treasury the power to require people to turn in all their gold coin, gold bullion, and gold certificates, on penalty of $10,000 fine and/or ten years in jail.

Notably, this act was called the "Bank Conservation Act" or the "Emergency Banking Act."

It was passed without individual congressmen even having the opportunity to read the bill.

Instant Replay and Analysis

Let us freeze the action here and replay it in slow motion with explanations. Remember the colonists' dilemma over money, minting, and banking in general? Recall that the constitution gave congress the power to coin money and establish its value.

The Federal Reserve Act was passed in 1913 authorizing creation of a central bank. The bank was, among other things, to be a secure vault for the gold of the people. People deposited their gold in the federal vault and were issued Federal Reserve notes, which said, in effect, that any time the depositor desired he could bring the note back to the bank and take back the same amount of gold that he had deposited.

Now the people were exercising that option. If the gold were still in the federal vaults, there should not have been a crisis. So what was the problem with giving the people back their gold?

In President Hoover's last days of office, he asked the banking institution, the Federal Reserve Board of New York, for recommendations. They responded, but President Hoover refused to act, saying their proposals were neither justified or necessary. What did the bankers request? Exactly what President Roosevelt proclaimed two days after he took office, before the congress had even met. In fact, the bankers included a proposed resolution, which was copied almost word for word in the president's Proclamation 2039.

There is evidence that the gold was not in the vaults. Wilber and Hyde in "Hoover Policies" say this:

"That these speculators and insiders were right was plain enough later on. This first contact of the 'moneychangers' with the New Deal netted those who removed their money from the country a profit of up to 60 percent when the dollar was debased."

President Roosevelt's Proclamation 2039 (as suggested by the bankers) began "Whereas there have been heavy and unwarranted withdrawals of gold and currency from our banking institutions for the purpose of hoarding..."

Stop and think about this. The people deposited the gold in the bank. They were issued a contractual certificate (federal reserve note) saying they could have their gold any time they presented the federal reserve note. Now many people were starving, living on the street or in shacks, begging handouts, and those that had gold in the bank wanted it back.

Yet the bankers' resolution claimed the withdrawals were unwarranted and for the purpose of hoarding. The bankers asked, in effect, to be let out of their contract to give back the gold to the rightful owners, the depositors, upon demand.

The bankers' resolution provided that anyone violating any provision of the act would be fined not more than $10,000 and jailed for not more than 10 years, or both. During the depression, a fine of $10,000 was staggering.

Proclamation 2040 stated "by virtue of the authority vested in me by Section 5(b) of the Act of October 6, 1917 (40 Stat. 1. 411) as amended by the Act of March 9, 1933, I do hereby proclaim, order, direct and declare that all the terms and provisions of said Proclamation of March 6, 1933, and the regulations and orders issued thereunder are hereby continued in full force and effect until further proclamation by the president." This proclamation was issued before the congress met, and before Section 5(b) of the Act of October 6, 1917 had even been considered for amendment, much less amended.

Trading With the Enemy Act

Following is the text of Section 2 and 5(b) of the Act of October 6, 1917, which is known as the Trading With the Enemy Act:

Section 2:

That the word "enemy" as used herein, shall be deemed, for the purpose of such trading and of this Act -- Any individual, partnership, or body of individuals residing within any nation with which the U.S. is at war.

"Ally of enemy" means any one who resides within a nation which is an ally with a nation with which the U.S. is at war."

Section 5(b)

That the President may investigate, regulate, or prohibit, under such rules and regulations as he may prescribe, by means of licenses or otherwise, any transactions in foreign exchange, export or earmarkings of gold or silver coin or bullion or currency, transfers of credit in any form (other than credits relating solely to transactions to be executed wholly within the United States), ...

It is clear that people and transactions wholly within the United States were specifically excluded from the war power of seizure under this Act. The American people were not enemies.

Congress Gives President Power to Do What He Has Already Done

However, the Emergency Banking Act that congress passed on March 9, 1933, amended Section 5(b) of the Trading with the Enemy Act to give the President approval to do the things he had already done.

Sec. 2. Subdivision (b) of section 5 of the Act of October 6, 1917 (40 Stat. L. 411), as amended, is hereby amended to read as follows:

"(b) During time of war or during any other period of national emergency declared by the President, the President may, through any agency that he may designate, or otherwise, investigate, regulate, or prohibit, under such rules and regulations as he may prescribe, by means of licenses or otherwise, any transactions in foreign exchange, transfers of credit between or payments by banking institutions as defined by the President, and export, hoarding, melting, or earmarking of gold or silver coin or bullion or currency, by any person within the United States or any place subject to the jurisdiction thereof; and the President may require any person engaged in any transaction referred to in this subdivision to furnish under oath, complete production of any books of account, contracts, letters or other papers, in connection therewith in the custody or control of such person, either before or after such transaction is completed. Whoever wilfully violates any of the provisions of this subdivision or of any license, order, rule or regulation issued thereunder, shall, upon conviction, be fined not more than $10,000 ..."

American People Defined as Enemy

With this Act, the Trading with the Enemy Act was expanded to include the American people and all commerce within the United States.

The American people were declared, in effect, to be the public enemy and were made subject to the total war powers of government. A constitutional dictatorship of total control over the economic and social agenda of the US was established.

The government now came "at the people" instead of "from the people."

Enemy's Money Seized (Enemy = American Citizens)

The banks, along with the people's money they held, were seized and closed by Department of Treasury orders.

Historically, the US had recognized two types of currency: gold and silver - the peacetime money, and paper - the war and emergency currency.

New Money Issued, Backed by Debt, Not Gold

> Roosevelt's papers said "...it was at first believed that some form of script or emergency currency would be necessary for the conduct of ordinary business... but after the passage of the Emergency Banking Act of March 9, 1933 (48 Stat. 1), it became evident that they would not be needed, because the act made possible the issue of the necessary amount of emergency currency in the form of Federal Reserve bank notes, which could be based on any sound assets owned by banks. (Roosevelt Papers, Vol. 2 p. 29)

The Federal Reserve notes after March 9, 1933, became Federal Reserve bank notes and were emergency war script. They were no longer backed by the gold of the people; all gold had been seized as an act of war. The Federal Reserve bank notes were now backed by the assets of the banks. The assets of the banks are the mortgages held on the people and their property.

Congress Recognizes New Money is Mortgage Against People's Property

Representative Patman explained the new system this way:

> "Under the new law the money is issued to the banks in return for government obligations, bills of exchange, drafts, notes, trade acceptances, and bankers acceptances. The money will be worth 100 cents on the dollar, because it is backed by the credit of the nation. It will represent a mortgage on all the homes, and other property of all the people in the nation."
>
> (Congressional Record, March 9, 1933 on HR 1491, p. 83)

Eavesdropping on Congressional Debate

Let us listen in on congressional debate on this act on March 9, 1933.

Mr. McGugin. If we start out printing currency without regard for the gold reserve, then in the end, when we find that excessive inflation destroys the country and the people, we shall try to get back to the gold standard. Then we shall find that we have so much currency outstanding that we cannot tie it to our limited supply of gold except by reducing the content of the gold dollar in proportion to the increased amount of currency. That may mean that we shall have to decrease the gold content 50 percent, maybe 15 percent, and maybe 90 percent. It will all depend on how far we carry the inflation during the period that our currency is not tied to gold. It may be that we shall do as Germany did by going so far that there is no possibility of tying all of our outstanding currency to gold, and we shall be obliged to repudiate and cancel some of our currency.

Anyone knows that this Government cannot now collect enough taxes to meet its present expenses. Whenever governments reach the position where they can neither collect enough taxes to meet their expenses nor borrow enough to meet their expenses, there is only one thing left for them, and that is to print money. Such is the position of the United States; and, whether we like it or not, there is going to be some inflation in order to meet the obligations of the Government.

Mr. Patman. The President submitted a bill which was intended to assist in the opening of all the banks in the Nation. Although it was contrary to many of the principles that I have advocated for many years, it contained provisions I do not approve and failed to go far enough in other ways. I yielded and voted for the bill; it was an emergency measure and should have been passed immediately. The proposal embodied one feature that I have advocated for a long time, and that was the issuance of additional circulating medium. The banks of the Nation have inflated credit out of proportion to the amount of actual money. The result is the banks have become indebted to their depositors to the extent of $45,000,000,000 and have in their vaults less than $1,000,000,000 to pay it with. The new law will cause the printing presses at the Bureau of Engraving and Printing here in Washington to print more money and furnish it to the banks.

Mr. McFadden. Mr. Speaker, I regret that the membership of the House has had no opportunity to consider or even read this bill. The first opportunity I had to know what this legislation is was when it was read from the Clerk's desk. It is an important banking bill. It is a dictatorship over finance in the United States. It is complete control over the banking system in the United States.

The first section of the bill, as I grasped it, is practically the war powers that were given back in 1917, with some slight amendments. The other gives supreme authority to the Secretary of the Treasury of the United States to impound all the gold in the United States....I would like to ask the chairman of the committee if this is a plan to change the holding of the security back of Federal Reserve notes to the treasury of the United States rather than the Federal Reserve agent.

Mr. Steagall. This provision is for the issuance of Federal Reserve bank notes; not for Federal Reserve notes; and the security back of it is the obligations, notes, drafts, bills of exchange, bank acceptances, outlined in the section to which the gentlemen has referred.

Mr. McFadden. Then the new circulation is to be Federal Reserve bank notes and not Federal Reserve notes? Is that true?

Mr. Steagall. Insofar as the provisions of this section are concerned, yes.

Mr. Britten. From my observation of the bill as it was read to the House, it would appear that the amount of bank notes that might be issued by the Federal Reserve System is not limited. That will depend entirely upon the amount of collateral that is presented from time to time for exchange for bank notes. Is that not correct?

Mr. McFadden. Yes. I think that is correct.

Mr. Britten. So that it might run to $20,000,000,000?

Mr. McFadden. In the discretion of the President and the Secretary of the Treasury. These notes are to be secured by assets that are approved, that are turned over by financial institutions to the Treasury of the United States.

[Applause.}

Congressional Record, March 9, 1933 p. 80

The Hundred Days

The following actions taken by President Roosevelt and congress were called "The Hundred Days."

March 9 - The Emergency Banking Act - complete control of all banks, gold and silver, currency and transactions.

March 20 - The Economy Act - an act to reduce the government deficit.

March 31 - Civil Conservation Act - an act to control use of natural resources.

April 19 - Abandonment of gold standard - seizure of all gold.

May 12 - Emergency Relief Act - control of social agenda and national welfare program.

May 12 - Agricultural Adjustment Act - an Act to nationalize and control all production and pricing of agricultural commodities.

May 18 - Tennessee Valley Authority - nationalization of utilities.

May 27 - Truth in Securities - control of private financing.

June 5 - House Joint Resolution 192 - abrogation of gold clause in public and private contracts - control of all contracts.

June 13 - Home Owner's Loan Act - control financing and prices of homes and bail out banks.

June 18 - National Industrial Recovery Act - nationalization of industry and labor. Provided for industrial self-government under federal control, and provided $3.3 billion for public works.

June 16 - Glass-Steagall Act - divorced commercial and investment banking and guaranteed bank deposits, and led to establishment of the FDIC.

June 16 - Railroad Coordination Act - resulted in nationalization of transportation.

State Owns All Property; People are Mere Users

Senate Document No. 43, 73rd Congress, 1st Session, states:

"The ownership of all property is in the State; individual so-called 'ownership' is only by virtue of Government, i.e., law, amounting to mere user; and use must be in accordance with law and subordinate to the necessities of the State."

America Has Been Nationalized

The first hundred days and subsequent acts provided for the complete nationalization of America. All of these acts were based on the wartime Trading With the Enemy Act, which had been amended to include the American people and all transactions within the nation.

Agricultural Adjustment Act Gives President Power over Money System

Oddly enough, the power given to congress by the constitution to coin money and regulate the value thereof, was transferred to the president in the Agricultural Adjustment Act of May 12, 1933. It states:

> Sec. 43. Whenever the President finds, upon investigation, that (1) the foreign commerce of the United States is adversely affected by reason of the depreciation in the value of the currency of any other government or government in relation to the present standard value of gold, or (2) action under this section is necessary in order to regulate and maintain the parity of currency issues of the United States, or (3) an economic emergency requires an expansion of credit, or (4) an expansion of credit is necessary to secure by international agreement a stabilization at proper levels of the currencies of various governments, the President is authorized, in his discretion ...
>
> (a)
>
> (b)
>
> (c)
>
> Sec (45) (g)
>
> Notwithstanding the foregoing provisions of this section, the Federal Reserve Board, upon the affirmative vote of not less than five of its members and with the approval of the President, may declare that an emergency exists by reason of credit expansion, and may by regulation during

such emergency increase or decrease from time to time, in its discretion, the reserve balances required to be maintained against either demand or time deposits.

Approved May 12, 1933.

Permanent Agency Created to Deal with Temporary Problem

The Agriculture Adjustment Act created a permanent agency, the Agricultural Adjustment Administration, to deal with a problem defined as temporary by the very nature of the authority used to create it - the war and emergency powers.

If Money Based on Debt Value, Value Must Be Propped Up

With this concept of currency based upon the assets of the people it became imperative that these assets be supported. This concept is explicitly defined in the Agricultural Adjustment Act:

"That the present acute economic emergency being in part the consequence of a severe and increasing disparity between the prices of agricultural and other commodities, which disparity has largely destroyed the purchasing power of farmers for industrial products, has broken down the orderly exchange of commodities, and has seriously impaired the agricultural assets supporting the national credit structure, it is hereby declared that these conditions in the basic industry of agriculture have affected transactions in agricultural commodities with a national public interest, have burdened and obstructed the normal currents of commerce in such commodities, and render imperative the immediate enactment of Title I of this Act."

Total Control Over Farm Prices Established

Arthur Schlesinger, Jr., interprets this farm move: "The board design was clear: to help correct the imbalance between industry and agriculture by raising farm prices; and to raise farm prices through the curtailment of production, the regulation of marketing, and a variety of other devices. And there was general agreement on the mechanism: the establishment of a new agency within the Department of Agriculture, to be called the Agriculture Adjustment Administration. But the immense discretion conferred on the Executive under the AAA law left many crucial decisions for the future. Much would therefore depend on the men summoned to conduct what Mordecai Ezekiel pronounced the greatest single experiment in economic planning under capitalist conditions ever attempted by a democracy in times of peace."

Home Owners Loan Act Props Up Property Values, Bails Out Banks

The Home Owners Loan Act was likewise adopted amidst cries that the act bailed out real estate interests rather than the home owner. Without having to scale down the debt he was owed, the mortgagor could turn defaulted mortgages for government -guaranteed bonds. The price of homes was thus arbitrarily supported at a high level.

With the price of land and homes arbitrarily supported, the banks could claim sound assets for which in return they could obtain Federal Reserve bank notes from the system.

It was through this method that the modern day "money" creation system was established.

Two Ways to Create Money

As government obligations were also authorized securities for the creation of Federal Reserve bank notes, there were thus two mechanisms established by which money could be created.

1. The people could go directly to the member banks and mortgage their property. These assets could be discounted to the Federal Reserve Banks for currency.

2. The government could mortgage the people and their property through government obligation and discount these directly to the Federal Reserve Bank.

Both methods were used extensively in order to encourage private mortgaging as much as possible. The Farm Credit Act and the Home Owners Loan Act were created in June of 1933.

The Securities Act of 1933 which established the Securities Exchange Commission gave the government control over all private securities and thus controlled all private means of financing. Many who could have previously financed privately were forced by this act into "public financing" which helped dramatically to expand the supply of currency.

The government also helped to expand the currency. This is shown in the annual budget message of January 3, 1934.

Two National Budgets

Roosevelt presented the financial position and budget::

"In my annual message to the congress I have already summarized the problems presented by the deflationary forces of the depression, the paralyzed condition which affected the banking system, business, agriculture, transportation, and, indeed, the whole orderly continuation of the

Nation's social and economic system. I have outlined the steps taken since last March for the resumption of normal activities and the restoration of the credit of the Government. Of necessity these many measures have caused spending by the Government far in excess of the income of the Government.

The results of expenditures already made show themselves in concrete form in better prices for farm commodities, in renewed business activity, in increased employment, in reopening of and restored confidence in banks, and in well - organized relief.

THE CURRENT FISCAL YEAR (Ending June 30, 1934)

Exclusive of debt retirement of $488,171,500 for this year, Budget estimates of expenditures, including operating expenses of the regular Government establishments and also all expenditures which may be broadly classed as caused by the necessity for recovery from the depression will amount this year (ending June 30, 1934) to $9,403,006,967. (See Budget Statement No. 3, Table A.) This total falls in broad terms into the following classifications:

Expenditures for fiscal year ending June 30, 1934

General:	
Departmental	$2,889,116,200
Legislative	17,718,500
Independent Establishments	616,857,067
	$3,533,691,767
Less public debt retirements	488,171,500
Total, general	$3,045,520,267
Emergency:	
Public Works Admn.	$1,611,190,800
Agricultural Adjustment Admn.	103,250,000
Farm Credit Admn.	40,000,000
Emergency Conservation Work	341,705,600
Reconstruction Finance Corp.	3,969,740,300
Tennessee Valley Authority	19,000,000
Federal Land Banks	52,350,000
Federal Deposit Ins. Corp.	150,000,000
Nat'l. Indus. Recovery Admn.	4,250,000
Total, emergency	$6,357,486,700
Total, general and emergency, less public debt retirement	$9,403,006,967

As against these expenditures, which have either been appropriated for or for which appropriations are asked, the estimated receipts for this fiscal year (ending June 30, 1934) are $3,259,938,756. (See Budget Statement No. 2, Table A.)

On this basis, including, however, certain additional expenditures for 1934 which are not included in the Budget estimates but which I believe to be necessary and amounting to $1,166,000,000 as shown in a subsequent table herein, the excess of expenditures over receipts will be $7,309,068,211. Interest charges on the borrowings in excess of Budget estimates will slightly increase this figure.

On the basis of these estimates, the public debt, in the strict sense of the term, at the expiration of this fiscal year will therefore amount to approximately $29,847,000,000, or an increase as shown above of $7,309,068,211.

However, as against this increase in the total debt figure, it is right to point out that the various governmental agencies have loans outstanding with a book value of $3,558,516,189 against which collateral or assets have been pledged.

In order to make clear to the congress what our borrowing problem is for the next 6 months, permit me to remind you that we shall have to borrow approximately 6 billion dollars of new money and, in addition, 4 billion dollars to meet maturities of a like amount.

Roosevelt Papers Vol. 3 p. 16-18

Full Service Government:
"We'll Mortgage Your Property For You.
Fast Service. No Forms."

From this message two things become clear: 1) two separate governments were operated and budgeted, the general government and the emergency Government; 2) the emergency government was funded through deficit spending. This deficit spending resulted in the borrowing of "New Money ."

Thus we see that the people could either mortgage themselves or be mortgaged by the government. Either way was immaterial as all money created by these mortgages were obligations upon the people.

Later that same year congress enacted legislation creating the Federal Deposit Insurance Corporation. This made the guarantee of all deposits in the banks obligations of the same people, the taxpayers. Thus if some of the sound assets of the banks failed, the losses were simply shifted to those sound assets that remained.

By now it should be quite obvious that the "sound assets" referred to, in all cases, are the people and their property.

We had become assets of the government; in short chattel property.

Trying to Borrow Our Way into Prosperity

The public debt in 1934 was approximately $29 billion with an annual deficit of approximately $1 billion. In 1993 the public debt had grown to $4 trillion with an annual deficit of $450 billion. The total public and private debt has been estimated at $14 trillion. The prosperity of the past has been based on debt. It was a false prosperity.

Where's the Gold?

The next question that should be asked is: "What happened to the people's gold which was seized?" The answer can be found in the Public Papers and Addresses of Roosevelt 1934, page 42.

Don't Worry. The Government Got It!

"Such legislation places the right, title, and ownership to our gold reserves in the Government itself; it makes clear the government ownership of any added dollar value of the country's stock of gold which would result from any decrease in the gold content of the dollar which may be made in the public interest.

"The title to all gold being in the government, the total stock will serve as a permanent and fixed metallic reserve which will change in amount only so far as necessary for the settlement of international balances or as may be required by a future agreement among the Nations of the World for a redistribution of the world stock of monetary gold."

We thus see the title to the people's gold was seized and passed into government hands. We also see that it was contemplated that the gold would be redistributed through some future agreement of the nations of the world. This came in 1945 in the form of the Bretton Woods Agreement.

During the Civil War the banks profited greatly with the issuance of paper war currency. People who had deposited gold into banks were required to accept deflated paper currency in return. The banks then sold the gold at greatly inflated prices. When asked the question "The profit from this operation clearly is to go to the Treasury?" the president responded:

The President: Yes. Right on that point, there has been a divergence of opinion amongst some of the bankers - not by any means all - and on the part of a few politicians who have wondered whether the Government had any right to take this profit or whether the profit should accrue to the stockholders of the banks. Of course, so far as I can see, there is no question on that at all. We asked individuals to turn in their gold and get paper money for it. We also asked all the corporations to do it, and substantially all did as requested. I cannot see a great deal of difference between a bank and a private corporation. The constituent bank is owned by private individuals, and if we were to pursue that policy of letting the stockholders of the banks take this profit, it would mean that the Government would be handing them a great big Christmas present.

Roosevelt Papers Vol. 3 ,p. 51-52

Taking the Gold was a Seizure Act of War

The Emergency Banking Act of 1933 thus varied from the act of the Civil War. The act of 1933 was a seizure act of war.

Shall We Take the Silver?

In a White House statement following a conference on silver policy, May 8, 1934 it is stated:

At a conference between a number of Senators, the Secretary of the Treasury and the President, there was further discussion of two points relating to the further use of silver as a metallic reserve for the United States.

More specifically, the possibility of nationalizing silver in the same manner in which gold has already been nationalized through the purchase of existing free stocks at a limited price was explored.

The meeting also explored the ultimate objective or national policy of having 25 percent of the monetary value of the metallic reserves of the country in the form of silver.

Roosevelt Papers Vol. 3, p. 216.

We see from this statement that gold was nationalized in 1933. Silver was subsequently nationalized by Executive Order No. 6814 on August 9, 1934. (Roosevelt Papers p. 378) and federal licenses were required, pursuant to the Trading With the Enemy Act of 1917 as amended. The nationalization of currency was now complete.

The only means left to the American people to acquire and use a medium of exchange was through mortgage debts upon themselves, their property and their posterity. The American people were placed in a permanent state of bondage - all through the war powers of government.

Farmers Enjoy New Status of Serfdom

Farmers fared no better than the rest of society. On March 11, 1933 Roosevelt was requested by some farm leaders to call upon congress :

"for the same broad powers to meet the emergency in agriculture as I had requested for solving the banking crisis. Three days later I sent the proposed bill, which had been drafted in accordance with recommendations of the conference. It was the most drastic and far-reaching piece of farm legislation ever proposed in time of Peace."

The same broad powers referred to were the war powers contained in the act of October 6, 1917 as amended.

By this act the government had authority to set prices, control production, regulate marketing, and in a variety of other devices, completely control agriculture.

Title II of the act (Agricultural Credits) provides various methods by which farmers could borrow new money into existence with government guarantees of performance. This title was instituted to provide soundness to the agriculture securities, which supported the new money and the national credit structure.

In Title III of the Agricultural Adjustment Act, congress transferred to the president its power to coin money and regulate its value.

When Does It End?

When the President Says So!

Termination of the Act (Sec. 13) states:

This title shall cease to be in effect whenever the President finds and proclaims that the national economic emergency in relation to agriculture has been ended; and pending such time the President shall by proclamation terminate with respect to any basic agricultural commodity such provisions of this title as he finds are not requisite to carrying out the declared policy with respect to such commodity. The Secretary of Agriculture shall make such investigations and reports thereon to the President as may be necessary to aid him in executing this section.

Agricultural Adjustment Act p. 39

Is It Over Yet?

This act created a permanent agency with permanent emergency war control of agriculture. There has been no presidential proclamation terminating this act to date.

Industry is Nationalized

Roosevelt recommended the National Industrial Recovery Act to Congress on May 17, 1933:

"Before the Special Session of the Congress adjourns, I recommend two further steps in our national campaign to put people to work.

"My first request is that the congress provide for the machinery necessary for a great cooperative movement throughout all industry in order to obtain wide reemployment, to shorten the working week, to pay a decent wage for the shorter week and to prevent unfair competition and disastrous overproduction.

"Employers cannot do this singly or even in organized groups, because such action increases costs and thus permits cut-throat underselling by selfish competitors unwilling to join in such a public spirited endeavor.

"One of the greatest restrictions upon such cooperative efforts up to this time has been our anti-trust laws. They were properly designed as the means to cure the great evils of monopolistic price fixing. They should certainly be retained as a permanent assurance that the old evils of unfair competition shall never return. But the public interest will be served if, with the authority and under the guidance of Government, private industries are permitted to make agreements and codes insuring fair competition. However, it is necessary, if we thus limit the operation of anti-trust laws to their original purpose, to provide a rigorous licensing power in order to meet rare cases of non-cooperation and abuse. Such a safeguard is indispensable.

Roosevelt Papers Vol. 2 p. 202

Cooperate and Buy Exemption from Antitrust Laws

This act mandated the price and hours of labor. Employers in return for paying the mandated price for shorter hours of labor were given exemption from the Sherman Antitrust Acts. Employers or businesses were in turn required to form trade associations and to formulate codes of practice among themselves insuring fair competition. These trade associations would later become the special interest groups.

The codes had to be approved by the president or by his representative. The code once approved was to become binding upon the entire industry to which it applied and was to be enforceable in court. Every code was required (by the now famous Section 1-A of the statute) to guarantee to employees the right of collective bargaining by representatives of their own choosing, free from restraint or coercion of employers.

Approved code activities were to be exempt from the antitrust laws.

The codes generally contained two general classes of provisions: (I). labor provisions and (2) trade practice provisions.

(From Roosevelt Papers Vol. 2 p. 246-247)

Roosevelt stated on June 16, 1933, "It seems to me to be equally apparent that no business which depends for existence on paying less than a living wage to its workers has any right to continue in this country .

"It is, further, a challenge to administration. We are relaxing some of the safeguards of the antitrust laws. The public must be protected against the abuses that led to their enactment, and to this end, we are putting in place of old principles of unchecked competition some new Government controls. They must, above all, be impartial and just. Their purpose is to free business, not to shackle it; and no man who stands on the constructive, forward-looking side of his industry has anything to fear from them. To such men the opportunities for individual initiative will open more amply than ever. Let me make it clear, however, that the antitrust laws still stand firmly against monopolies that restrain trade and price fixing which allows inordinate profits or unfairly high prices.

"If we ask our trade groups to do that which exposes their business, as never before, to undermining by members who are unwilling to do their part, we must guard those who play the game for the general good against those who may seek selfish gains from the unselfishness of others. We must protect them from the racketeers who invade organizations of both employers and workers. We are spending billions of dollars and if that spending is really to serve our ends it must be done quickly. We must see that our haste does not permit favoritism and graft. All this is a heavy load for any Government and one that can be borne only if we have the patience, cooperation, and support of people everywhere.

"Finally, this law is a challenge to our whole people. There is no power in America that can force against the public will such action as we require. But there is no group in America that can withstand the force of an aroused public opinion. This great cooperation can succeed only if those who bravely go forward to restore jobs have aggressive public support and those who lag are made to feel the full weight of public disapproval.

"As to the machinery, we shall use the practical way of accomplishing what we are setting out to do. When a trade association has a code ready to submit and the association has qualified as truly representative, and after reasonable notice has been issued to all concerned, a public hearing will be held by the Administrator or a deputy. A Labor Advisory Board appointed by the Secretary of Labor will be responsible that every affected labor group, whether organized or unorganized, is fully and adequately represented in an advisory capacity and any increased labor group will be entitled to be heard through representatives of its own choosing. An Industrial Advisory Board appointed by the Secretary of Commerce will be responsible that every affected industrial group is fully and adequately represented in an advisory capacity and any interested industrial group will be entitled to be heard through representatives of its own choosing. A Consumers Advisory Board will be responsible that the interests of the consuming public will be represented and every reasonable opportunity will be given to any group or class who may be affected directly or indirectly to present their views.

"At the conclusion of these hearings and after the most careful scrutiny by a competent economic staff the Administrator will present the subject to me for my action under the law.

"I am fully aware that wage increases will eventually raise costs, but I ask that managements give first consideration to the improvement of operating figures by greatly increased sales to be expected from the rising purchasing power of the public. That is good economics and good business. The aim of this whole effort is to restore our rich domestic market by raising its vast consuming capacity. If we now inflate prices as fast and as far as we increase wages, the whole project will be set at naught. We cannot hope for the full effect of this plan unless, in these first critical months, and, even at the expense of full initial profits, we defer price increases as long as possible. If we can thus start a strong, sound, upward spiral of business activity, our industries will have little doubt of black-ink operations in the last quarter of this year.

"The pent-up demand of this people is very great and if we can release it on so broad a front, we need not fear a lagging recovery. There is greater danger of too much feverish speed."

Roosevelt Papers Vol. 2 p. 253 - 255

So What If It's Not Constitutional?

As a British editorial put it:

"We did more under a code in one day than they in England had been able to do under the common law in eighty-five years of effort."

(Roosevelt Papers Vol. 2, p. 297)

The reason should be obvious; it couldn't be done under the common law as it was unconstitutional and in violation of the law of the land.

Compliance Enforced by Ostracism, Economic Sanctions

In connection with this agreement the Blue Eagle was devised as an official symbol to be used only by those who were operating under approved codes or who had signed the President's Reemployment Agreement. Patriotic citizens were expected to patronize only those concerns which displayed the Blue Eagle. The withdrawal of the right to display the Blue Eagle thus became an important method to enforce compliance.

Roosevelt Papers Vol. 2, p. 312

Code compliance was made a condition for government purchases and contracts. Executive Order No. 6246, August 10, 1933 provided:

"If the contractor fails to comply with the foregoing provisions (code authority), the government may by written notice to the contractor terminate the contractor's right to proceed with the contract, and the contractor and his sureties shall be liable to the government for any cost occasioned the government thereby ."

In an address at Vassar College on August 26, 1933 Roosevelt made the following observations:

"In the old days, when there were only agricultural communities, it was unfair, for example, to our neighbors to allow our cattle to roam on our neighbors' land. We were told we had to fence in our cattle.

"And then when we got into great cities it became unfair to maintain, let us say, a pigsty on Main and Market Streets.

"As this principle was extended, it became unfair to our neighbors if we - any individual or association of individuals - sought to make unfair profits from monopolies in things that everybody had to use, such as gas and electric lights and railroad tickets and freight rates and things of that kind.

"Still later on, it became uniformly accepted throughout the country, almost, that it was not fair to our neighbors to let anybody hire their children when they were little bits of things, when they ought to be at school, and especially that it was unfair to hire them at pitiful wages and with long hours of work.

"Many years ago we went even further in saying that the government - state government or national government - would have the right to impose increasing taxes on increasing profits because of a simple principle that very large profits were made at the expense of neighbors and, therefore, should at least to some extent be used through taxes for the benefit of the neighbors."

Roosevelt Papers Vol. 2, p. 340 - 341

President Hints of Income Tax Enactment

In his second "Fireside Chat" of September 30, 1934, Roosevelt hinted at a graduated income tax. He stated:

"We have passed through the formative period of code making in the National Recovery Administration and have effected a reorganization of the N.R.A. suited to the needs of the next phase, which is, in turn, a period of preparation for legislation which will determine its permanent form.

"In this recent reorganization we have recognized three distinct functions: first, the legislative or policy-making function; second, the administrative function of code making and revision; and, third, the judicial function, which includes enforcement, consumer complaints and the settlement of disputes between employers and employees and between one employer and another.

"We are now prepared to move into this second phase, on the basis of our experience in the first phase under the able and energetic leadership of General Johnson.

President Hints of Permanent Nationalization

"We shall watch carefully the working of this new machinery for the second phase of N.R.A., modifying it where it needs modification and finally making recommendations to the congress, in order that the functions of N.R.A. which have proved their worth may be made a part of the permanent machinery of government.

"Let me call your attention to the fact that the National Industrial Recovery Act gave business men the opportunity they had sought for years to improve business conditions through what has been called self-government in industry. If the codes which have been written have been too complicated, if they have gone too far in such matters as price fixing and limitation of production, let it be remembered that so far as possible, consistent with the immediate public interest of this past year and the vital necessity of improving labor conditions, the representatives of trade and industry were permitted to write their ideas into the codes.

"Another question arises as to whether in fixing minimum wages on the basis of an hourly or weekly wage we have reached into the heart of the problem which is to provide such annual earnings for the lowest paid worker as will meet his minimum needs. We also question the wisdom of extending code requirements suited to the great industrial centers and to large employers, to the great number of small employers in the smaller communities.

"When the business men of the country were demanding the right to organize themselves adequately to promote their legitimate interests; when the farmers were demanding legislation which would give them opportunities and incentives to organize themselves for a common advance, it was natural that the workers should seek and obtain a statutory declaration of their constitutional right to organize themselves for collective bargaining as embodied in Section 1-A of the National Industrial Recovery Act."

President Defends Actions

"Those, fortunately few in number, who are frightened by boldness and cowed by the necessity for making decisions, complain that all we have done is unnecessary and subject to great risks. Now that these people are coming out of their storm cellars, they forget that there ever was a storm. They point to England. They would have you believe that England has made progress out of her depression by a do-nothing policy, by letting nature take her course. England has her peculiarities and we have ours, but I do not believe any intelligent observer can accuse England of undue orthodoxy in the present emergency."

"Did England let nature take her course? No. Did England hold to the gold standard when her reserves were threatened? No. Has England gone back to the gold standard today? No. Did England hesitate to call in ten billion dollars of her war bonds bearing 5 percent interest, to issue new bonds therefor bearing only 3 1/2 percent interest, thereby saving the British Treasury one hundred and fifty million dollars a year in interest alone? No. And let it be recorded that the British bankers helped. Is it not a fact that ever since the year 1909, Great Britain in many ways has advanced further along lines of social security than the United States? Is it not a fact that relations between capital and labor on the basis of collective bargaining are much further advanced in Great Britain than in the United States? It is perhaps not strange that the conservative British press has told us with pardonable irony that much of our New Deal program is only an attempt to catch up with English reforms that go back ten years or more.

"More than twenty-one years ago, when Theodore Roosevelt and Woodrow Wilson were attempting to correct abuses in our national life, the great Chief Justice White said: 'There is great danger it seems to me to arise from the constant habit which prevails where anything is opposed or objected to, of referring without rhyme or reason to the constitution as a means of preventing its accomplishment, thus creating the general impression that the constitution is but a barrier to progress instead of being the broad highway through which lone true progress may be enjoyed.'

"I am not for a return to that definition of liberty under which for many years a free people were being gradually regimented into the service of the privileged few. I prefer and I am sure you prefer that broader definition of liberty under which we are moving forward to greater freedom, to greater security for the average man than he has ever known before in the history of America.

Roosevelt Papers Vol. 3, p. 417- 422

President Doesn't Let Constitution Stand in Way

Roosevelt obviously believed the constitution should not act as a barrier to his economic and social agenda. The N. R. A., an executive agency, was empowered with the executive, legislative, and judicial functions in direct violation of the separation of powers doctrine of the constitution.

What is a Tyranny?

Madison had defined a tyranny in the Federalist Papers XLVII:

"The accumulation of all powers, legislative, executive, and judiciary, in the same hands, whether of one, a few, or many, and whether hereditary, self appointed, or elective, may justly be pronounced the very definition of tyranny."

The Supreme Court agreed with Madison.

Supreme Court Declares Acts Unconstitutional

From Roosevelt Papers:

The first major case which sought to break down our attempts to cure the abuses and inequalities and instability which had thrown our economic system out of joint involved the provisions of the National Industrial Recovery Act, which conferred on the President the power to prohibit the transportation in interstate commerce of petroleum which had been produced in excess of the quantity permitted by the respective state laws (see Items 30, 62, 95, 95A of Vol. II). These provisions were inserted to enable the Federal Government to cope with the chaotic conditions in the oil industry which the states themselves had proved powerless to meet. Continued overproduction and price-cutting, in the face of decreasing demand, had made it necessary for the Federal Government to step in and place the industry on a sound basis by lending its power to prevent overproduction of oil in the various states which, by themselves, had been unable to prevent it.

National Industrial Recovery Act Ruled Unconstitutional

The decision of the Court, which was handed down on January 1, 1935, was that the act was unconstitutional as a delegation to the President of legislative power. The contentions of the Government that the statute constituted a valid regulation of interstate commerce and that there was no unconstitutional delegation of legislative power to the Executive, were overruled, Mr. Justice Cardozo vigorously dissenting.

Panama Refining Co. v. Bran, 293 U.S. 388.

New Monetary System Squeaks by Supreme Court by One Vote

A month later, February 18, 1935, came the Gold-Clause Cases 294 U.S. 240. These cases involved the validity of the Congressional Joint Resolution of June 5, 1933, which abrogated the gold clause in all Government and private contracts and provided that such obligations might be discharged by the payment of regular legal-tender currency. The Government contended that the Resolution was a valid exercise of the power of the congress over the currency system. By a bare vote of five to four, the Court sustained the contention of the Government and upheld the Resolution so far as private obligations were concerned. The Court held, however, that the abrogation of the gold clause as to Government obligations was not valid, but that the holders of Government bonds were not damaged by the abrogation of the gold clause and that therefore they were not entitled to recover. Mr. Justice Stone vigorously protested that since no damage had been proved, there was no occasion for the Court to question the validity of the Joint Resolution in its application to Government obligations and that the Court's decision might needlessly interpose serious obstacles to the adoption of measures for the stabilization of the dollar.

A difference of one vote in the case involving private obligations would have meant that the entire currency program and the entire gold and silver policy of the Government, which were among the chief foundations of the whole recovery program, would have been invalidated, that the pre-existing chaos in foreign exchange and domestic currency and the whole unfair debt structure would have returned, and that a favored few would have been unfairly enriched at the expense of the general public.

Railroad Retirement Act Ruled Unconstitutional

The next major Supreme Court decision, handed down on May 6, 1935, involved the Railroad Retirement Act (see Item 120, Vol. III). That act provided for the creation of a pooled fund to which contributions were to be made by all interstate railroads, for the purpose of paying pensions to retired railroad employees. The Government contended that the statute was a valid exercise of the power to regulate interstate commerce. The Court by a five to four decision held that the act deprived the railroads of property without due process of law in contravention of the Fifth Amendment; and also held that the statute was not a legitimate exercise of the power to regulate interstate commerce, since the provision for retirement and pensioning of aged employees has no reasonable relation to the business of interstate transportation.

Railroad Retirement Board v. Alton Railroad Co., 295 U.S. 330.

Code Making Provisions of NIRA Struck Down

During the same month, May 21, 1935, the Supreme Court by a unanimous decision struck down all the code-making provisions of the National Industrial Recovery Act (see Items 59, 78, 79, 81, 93, and 105 of Vol. II). These provisions authorized the President to approve codes of fair competition for various industries upon application by those industries.

The case involved a violation of the live poultry code by defendants whose business was to buy from concerns in New York State poultry which had been sent into New York State from other states, and who slaughtered the poultry for sale to retailers in New York. The charge against the defendants was that they violated the provisions of the code which fixed minimum wages and maximum hours and which set up certain trade practices to prevent unfair competition. The Government contended that this statute constituted a valid exercise of the power to regulate interstate commerce on the ground that the trade practices and the provisions for hours and wages have a direct effect on the price structure and the quality and volume of live poultry shipped in interstate commerce into New York; that they have particularly an effect on the interstate competition existing between the live poultry business and the dressed poultry business; that the intrastate transactions are so interwoven with interstate commerce that adequate control of the latter required control of the former; and that the act did not improperly delegate legislative power to the Executive, in view of the fact that it contained a statement of policies and standards under which the President must act.

The Supreme Court, however, held the statute unconstitutional on the grounds, first, that the code-making power sought to be conferred on the President was an invalid application of legislative power; and second, that the particular transactions involved in the case before it did not constitute interstate commerce.

A.L.A. Schechters Poultry Corp. v. United States, 295 U.S. 495.

Agricultural Adjustment Act Ruled Unconstitutional

The next major adversarial decision was a declaration of unconstitutionality of the Agricultural Adjustment Act on January 6, 1936. This act was enacted to help the farmers protect themselves by cooperative action against the accumulation of farm surpluses which had brought about disastrous farm prices and had left agriculture practically prostrate throughout the country. The statute provided for raising taxes on the processing of farm commodities and for appropriating the proceeds of the taxes to pay benefits to farmers who cooperated in adjusting their crop surpluses (see Items 20 and 54 of Vol. II).

The Government contended that the general welfare clause of the constitution (which gives the congress power "to lay and collect Taxes, Duties, Imposts and Excises, to... provide for the...general Welfare of the United States" should be construed broadly to include anything conducive to the national welfare, unaffected by the specifically enumerated powers which follow the clause; that pursuant to it, the congress may raise taxes and appropriate the proceeds to promote the national welfare. It urged that the determination of what was a national purpose rests with the congress and not with the courts and that the purposes of the act were in fact for the general welfare of the United States.

The Supreme Court held that the act was essentially one regulating agricultural production; that the processing tax was not really for raising revenue but was a mere incident of such regulation; that agricultural production is "a purely local activity"; that the general welfare clause of the constitution conferred on the congress the power to spend money in respect of any subject which pertained to the general welfare of the Nation without being limited by the specifically enumerated grants of congressional power; but that it did not extend to the use of the spending power for the purpose of regulating agricultural production which was a matter that pertained only to the local welfare as an intrastate activity.

United States v. Butler, 29b U.S. 1.

It was in this case that a dissenting opinion in which Mr. Justice Brandeis and Mr. Justice Cardozo joined (page 87), pointed out that such "a tortured construction of the constitution is not to be justified" and that the "Courts are not the only agency of government that must be assumed to have capacity to govern."

Bituminous Coal Conservation Act Ruled Unconstitutional

On May 18, 1936, came the next major adverse decision, in the opinion declaring unconstitutional the Bituminous Coal Conservation Act of 1935 (generally known as the first Guffey Coal Act, see Item 91, this volume). This statute was enacted to bring order out of chaos in the bituminous coal industry. The act provided for the fixing of minimum and maximum prices of coal, for a labor board to adjust labor disputes, for collective bargaining by employees through their own chosen representatives, for wages and hours to be mandatory upon the entire industry, if fixed by contracts between certain percentages of employers and employees.

The Government contended that the power to regulate interstate commerce included the power to regulate "price at the mine" in interstate commerce transactions and that therefore such price-fixing clauses of the act were valid. It further contended that the labor provisions of the act controlling the conditions under which coal is to be mined before it become an article of commerce were valid because they were designed to prevent strikes and other evils of production which directly affect interstate commerce in coal; but that if they were held to be invalid they were, in any event, separable provisions and their invalidity did not affect the validity of the price-fixing provisions.

The Court by a six to three vote held the labor provisions bad not on one but on three counts - bad as an unwarranted delegation of legislative power, bad as a violation of due process, bad as a regulation of intrastate commerce not within the purview of the commerce power. Five of the Justices plainly stated that the mining of coal is purely a local activity and not interstate commerce; that the whole relation between employers and employees with respect to wages, hours, working conditions and collective bargaining is purely a local one; and that mining, manufacturing, and farming are all local in character, no matter what is done with the products mined, manufactured or farmed, even if they be shipped into, and sold in, forty-seven other states.

The Court, without deciding the question as to whether the price-fixing provisions of the act were constitutional or not, held (by a majority vote) that they were not separable from the labor provisions, and that therefore the entire scheme of regulation fell.

Carter v. Carter Coal Co., 298 U.S. 238.

New York Minimum Wage Law Ruled Unconstitutional

Perhaps the climax of this line of decisions by the Supreme Court came on June 1, 1936, in the decision declaring unconstitutional, by a vote of five to four, the New York State Minimum Wage Law.

Morehead v. New York ex red. Tipaldo, 298 U.S. 587.
Roosevelt Papers Vol. 4, p. 1-12

"The Court Disapproves"

So in a year and half commencing with the "hot oil" case and ending with the New York minimum wage case the Supreme Court arrested the socialist war agenda of the government with a barrier which read: "The Court disapproves." (Roosevelt Papers Vol. 3, p. 13).

Court Says Emergency or Not, It's Unconstitutional. Roosevelt Fights Back

Roosevelt did not take these decisions lying down.

"Now, coming down to the decision itself. What are the implications? For the benefit of those of you who haven't read it through I think I can put it this way: the implications of this decision are much more important than almost certainly any decision of my lifetime or yours, more important than any decision probably since the Dred Scott case, because they bring the country as a whole up against a very practical question. That is in spite of what one gentleman said in the paper this morning, that I resented the decision. Nobody resents a Supreme Court decision. You can deplore a Supreme Court decision, and you can point out the effect of it. You can call the attention of the country to what the implications are as to the future, what the results of that decision are if future decisions follow this decision.

"Now take the decision itself. In the Schechter case the first part of it states the facts in the case, which you all know. Then it takes up the code itself and it points out that the code was the result of an act of congress. It mentions in passing that the act of congress was passed in a great emergency and that it sought to improve conditions immediately through the establishing of fair practices, through the prevention of unfair practices. It then goes on in general and says that even though it was an emergency, it did not make any difference whether it was an emergency or not, it was unconstitutional because it did not set forth very clearly, in detail, definitions of the broad language which was used in the act. In fact, it says that it makes no difference what kind of emergency this country ever gets into, an act has to be constitutional. Of course, it might take a month or two of delay to make an act constitutional and then you wouldn't know whether it was constitutional or not - you would have to do the best you could.

"Now, they have pointed out in regard to this particular act that it was unconstitutional because it delegated certain powers which should have been written into the act itself. And then there is this interesting language that bears that out. It is on page eight.

"We are told that the provisions of the statute authorizing the adoption of the codes must be viewed in the light of the grave national crisis with which congress was confronted. Undoubtedly, the conditions to which power is addressed are always to be considered when the exercise of power is challenged. Extraordinary conditions may call for extraordinary remedies. But the argument necessarily stops short of an attempt to justify action which lies outside the sphere of constitutional authority. Extraordinary conditions do not create or enlarge constitutional power."

Roosevelt Cites What President Did During WWI as Defense

"Of course, that is a very interesting implication. Some of us are old enough to remember the war days - the legislation that was passed in April, May and June of 1917.

"Being a war, that legislation was never brought before the Supreme Court. Of course, as a matter of fact, a great deal of that legislation was far more violative of the strict interpretation of the constitution than any legislation that was passed in 1933. All one has to do is to go back and read those war acts which conferred upon the Executive far greater power over human beings and over property than anything that was done in 1933.

Roosevelt Papers Vol. 4 p. 205-206

President Tries to Pack the Court

Roosevelt took immediate action to increase the number of justices on the Supreme Court. He rationalized that if he could get the number of justices increased, then he could appoint justices of his political belief and get the court to reverse their decisions. This led to cries that Roosevelt was attempting "to stack the court." Congress did not increase the number of justices, but it proved immaterial in the end. Due to resignation and death Roosevelt was able to appoint enough justices to control the court.

Court Reverses Decisions; Says Constitution is "Evolutionary Document"

In 1937-38 the Supreme Court reversed their previous rulings and the peacetime constitutional barriers to the socialist war time agenda were removed. The "original understanding" doctrine was replaced with the doctrine that the constitution was an "evolutionary document."

Every Industry is Regulated and Required to be Licensed

These codes were incorporated into the Codes of Federal Regulations (CFR). The CFR now controls virtually every industry or trade practice and every element of that industry or trade practice in the United States. Virtually every industry or trade practice is now required to be licensed and controlled under this authority. It amounted to nationalization of labor and industry.

The papers, emergency acts, proclamations, executive orders and Supreme Court decisions of the Roosevelt emergency government are too numerous to discuss within the scope of this book. To give the reader a flavor of the complete transformation of the form of government, a few will be noted. Aside from those actions noted previously, known as the "hundred days", there were many others of equal significance.

Regulation of Interstate Commerce of Petroleum. Executive Order No. 6199, July 11, 1933

By virtue of the authority vested in me by the act of congress entitled "An act to encourage national industrial recovery, to foster fair competition, and to provide for the construction of certain useful public works, and for other purposes," approved June 16, 1933 (Public No. 67, 73d Congress), the transportation in interstate and foreign commerce of petroleum and the products thereof produced or withdrawn from storage in excess of the amount permitted to be produced or withdrawn from storage by any state law or valid regulation or order prescribed thereunder, by any board, commission, officer, or other duly authorized agency of a state, is hereby prohibited.

Roosevelt Papers Vol. 2, p. 281

Power Given to the Secretary of the Interior to Enforce the Preceding Order, Executive Order No. 6204. July 14, 1933. By virtue of the authority vested in me by the act of congress entitled "An act to encourage national industrial recovery, to foster fair competition, and to provide for the construction of certain useful public works, and for other purposes," approved June 16, 1933 (Public No. 67, 73d Congress), in order to effectuate the intent and purpose of the congress as expressed in Section 9(c) thereof, and for the purpose of securing the enforcement of my order of July 11, 1933, issued pursuant to said act, I hereby authorize the Secretary of the Interior to exercise all the powers vested in me, for the purpose of enforcing Section 9C of said act and said order, including full authority to designate and appoint such agents and to set up such boards and agencies as he may see fit, and to promulgate such rules and regulations as he may deem necessary.

Note: The foregoing Executive Order authorized the Secretary of the Interior to exercise the authority granted to the President by Sections 9C of the National Industrial Recovery Act, with respect to interstate commerce in illegally produced oil.

The Secretary of the Interior the next day issued general rules and regulations to carry out the Federal statute.

Roosevelt Papers Vol. 2 p. 282

This order was declared unconstitutional in the "hot oil" case of 1935 but reversed with the stacked court of 1937.

President Decides to Redistribute Population

Delegation of Presidential Powers to the Secretary of the Interior Relating to Subsistence Homesteads. Executive Order No 6209.

NOTE: The foregoing Executive Order was issued pursuant to Section 208 of the National Industrial Recovery Act (see Items 78, 79, and 81 of this volume), which appropriated funds for the President to undertake a program of assisting in the establishment of subsistence homesteads, in order to aid in "the redistribution of the over-balance of population in industrial centers."

Roosevelt Papers Vol 2, p. 290-291

President Establishes Census Bureau

Establishment of a Central Statistical Board. Executive Order No. 6225. July 21, 1933

Roosevelt Papers Vol. 2, p. 307

These statistics were deemed necessary to effectively carry on the emergency government. The Functions, Powers and Regulations of the Public Works Administration. Executive Order No. 6252. Aug. 19, 1933

President Delegates Newfound Powers to Presidential Agencies

A. Delegation of Functions and Powers Pursuant to the authority vested in me by Section 201(a) of the National Industrial Recovery Act, approved June 16, 1933, I hereby delegate to the Federal Emergency Administrator of Public Works the following functions and powers:

1. To establish such agencies, to accept and utilize such voluntary and uncompensated services, and to utilize such Federal officers and employees and, with the consent of the state, such state and local officers and employees as he may find necessary, and to prescribe their authorities, duties, responsibilities, and tenure.

2. Under the conditions prescribed in Section 203 of said act, to construct, finance, or aid in the construction or financing of any public works project included in the program prepared pursuant to Section 202 of said act; upon such terms as he shall prescribe, to make grants to states, municipalities, or other public bodies for the construction, repair, or improvement of any such project; to acquire by purchase, or by exercise of the power of eminent domain, any real or personal property in connection with the construction of any such project and to lease any such property with or without the privilege of purchase; and to aid in the financing of such railroad maintenance and equipment as may be approved by the Interstate Commerce Commission as desirable for the improvement of transportation facilities.

Roosevelt Papers Vol. 2, p. 329

Commodity Credit Corporation Formed by Executive Order

Formation of the Commodity Credit Corporation. Executive Order No. 6340. October 16, 1933

Whereas, the congress of the United States has declared that an acute emergency exists by reason of widespread distress and unemployment, disorganization of industry, and the impairment of the agricultural assets supporting the national credit structure, all of which affects the national public interest and welfare, and Whereas, in order to meet the said emergency and to provide the relief necessary to protect the general welfare of the people, the congress of the United States has enacted the following acts:

1. The Agricultural Adjustment Act, approved May 12, 1933.

2. The National Industrial Recovery Act, approved June 16, 1933.

3. The Federal Emergency Relief Act of 1933, approved May 12, 1933.

4. Reconstruction Finance Corporation Act, approved January 22, 1932.

5. The Federal Farm Loan Act, approved July 17, 1916.

6. The Farm Credit Act of 1933, approved June 16, 1933.

7. The Emergency Relief and Construction Act of 1932, approved July 21, 1932.

Incorporation Papers Say CCC Stock Held by United States

The Commodity Credit Corporation was created under the laws of Delaware on the day following the foregoing Executive Order. It was extended to April 1, 1937, by act of Congress, Pub. No. 1, 74th Congress, approved January 31, 1935 (49 Stat. 1); and to June 30, 1939, by act of Congress, Pub. No. 2, 75th Congress, approved Jan. 26, 1937.

Its entire capital stock of $3,000,000 was subscribed and held by the Secretary of Agriculture and the Governor of the Farm Credit Administration on behalf of the United States. Pursuant to the act of April 10, 1936 (49 Stat. 1191), the capital stock was increased to $100,000,000, the R.F.C. acquiring the additional $97,000,000. The Corporation was authorized to make loans upon such farm commodities as might from time to time be designated by the President....

Roosevelt Papers Vol. 2, p. 404-407

Civil Work Administration Created by Executive Order

Executive Order No. 6420 B Creating Civil Work Administration to put 4,000,000 unemployed to work, Nov. 8, 1933

Federal Alcohol Control Administration Created

Executive Order No. 6474 Dec. 4, 1933 - The establishment of the Federal Alcohol Control Administration.

President Reduces Weight of Gold Dollar by 40%; Profit Pocketed by US Treasury

White House Statement on Presidential Proclamation No. 2072 Fixing the Weight of the Gold Dollar. January 31, 1934

1. Acting under the powers granted by Title 3 of the act approved May 12, 1933 (Thomas Amendment to the Farm Relief Act), the President today issued a Proclamation fixing the weight of the gold dollar at 15 5/21 grains nine-tenths fine. This is 59.06 plus percent of the former weight of 25 8/10 grains, nine-tenths fine, as fixed by Section 1 of the act of congress of March 4, 1900. The new gold content of the dollar became effective immediately on the signing of the Proclamation by the President. Under the Gold Reserve Act of 1934, signed by the President Tuesday, January 30th, title to the entire stock of monetary gold in the United States, including the gold coin and gold bullion heretofore held by the Federal Reserve Banks and the claim upon gold in the Treasury represented by gold certificates, is vested in the United States Government, and the "profit" from the reduction of the gold content of the dollar, made effective by today's Proclamation, accrues to the United States Treasury. Of this "profit" two billion dollars, under the terms of the Gold Reserve Act of today's Proclamation, constitute a

stabilization fund under the direction of the Secretary of the Treasury. The balance will be converted into the general fund of the Treasury. Settlement for the gold coin, bullion and certificates taken over from the Federal Reserve Banks on Tuesday upon the approval of the act was made in the form of credits set up on the Treasury's books. This credit due the Federal Reserve Banks is to be paid in the new form of gold certificates now in course of production by the Bureau of Engraving and Printing. These certificates bear on their face the wording:

"This is to certify that there is on deposit in the Treasury of the United States of America dollars in gold, payable to bearer on demand as authorized by law."

"They also will carry the standard legal tender clause, which is as follows:

"This certificate is a legal tender in the amount thereof in payment of all debts and dues, public and private."

The new gold certificates will be of the same size as other currency in circulation and the only difference, other than the changes in wording noted above, is that the backs of the new certificates will, as used to be done, be printed in yellow ink. The certificates will be in denominations up to $100,000.

Roosevelt Papers Vol. 3, p. 64-65

Export-Import Bank of Washington Is Created

Executive Order No. 6581 February 2, 1934

Whereas the congress of the United States has declared that a national emergency exists by reason of widespread unemployment and disorganization of industry; and has declared it to be the policy of congress to remove obstacles to the free flow of interstate and foreign commerce which tend to diminish the amount thereof, to provide for the general welfare, by promoting the fullest possible utilization of the present productive capacities of industries, to reduce and relieve unemployment, to improve standards of labor, and otherwise to rehabilitate industry; and Whereas in order to meet said emergency and to provide the relief necessary to protect the general welfare of the people the congress has enacted, *inter alia*, the following acts:

1. National Industrial Recovery Act, approved June 16, 1933:

2. Reconstruction Finance Corporation Act, approved January 22, 1932:

3. Bank Conservation Act, approved March 9, 1933; and Whereas in order effectively and efficiently to carry out the provisions of said acts it is expedient and necessary that a banking corporation be organized with power to aid in financing and to facilitate exports and imports and the exchange of commodities between the United States and other Nations or the agencies or nationals thereof;

Now, therefore, under and by virtue of the authority vested in me by the National Industrial Recovery Act of June 16, 1933, it is hereby declared that an agency, to wit: a banking corporation, be created pursuant to Title 5, Chapter 9, Section 261 of the Code of the District of Columbia, under the name of Export-Import Bank of Washington.

Roosevelt Papers Vol. 3, p. 76-77

President Establishes Control over Communications

Federal Communications Commission Public No. 416, 73rd Congress, 48 Stat. 1064. June 19, 1934

I have long felt that for the sake of clarity and effectiveness the relationship of the Federal Government to certain services known as utilities should be divided into three fields - transportation, power and communications. The problems of transportation are vested in the Interstate Commerce Commission, and the problems of power, its development, transmission and distribution, in the Federal Power Commission.

In the field of communications, however, there is today no single Government agency charged with broad authority.

The congress has vested certain authority over certain forms of communications in the Interstate Commerce Commission and there is in addition the agency known as the Federal Radio Commission.

I recommend that the congress create a new agency to be known as the Federal Communications Commission, such agency to be vested with the authority now lying in the Federal Radio Commission and with such authority over communications as now lies with the Interstate Commerce Commission - the services affected to be all of those which rely on wires, cables or radio as a medium of transmission.

It is my thought that a new Commission such as I suggest might well be organized this year by transferring the present authority of the Radio Commission and the Interstate Commerce Commission for the control of communications. The new body should, in addition, be given full power to investigate and study the business of existing companies and make recommendations to the congress for additional legislation at the next session.

Roosevelt Papers Vol. 3, p. 107-108

President Regulates Trade with Other Countries

Reciprocal Trade Agreement Act, June 12, 1934
Roosevelt stated:

"Legislation such as this is an essential step in the program of national economic recovery which the congress has elaborated during the past year. It is part of an emergency program necessitated by the economic crisis through which we are passing."

Roosevelt Papers Vol. 3, p. 115

No Compliance = No Government Contracts

Executive Order No. 6646 March 14, 1934

The Government Does Business Only with Those Complying with N.R.A. Codes.

Roosevelt Papers Vol. 3, p. 143

National Housing Act Established

National Housing Act June 21, 1934, Public No. 479, 73d Congress, 48 Stat. 1246

Note: The Federal Housing Administration set up by the statute does not loan its own money or make any grant of federal funds. What it does is to insure loans made by banks, building and loan associations, insurance companies and other private lending institutions for refinancing existing houses, for the construction of new homes and for the modernization and repair of all types of structures.

Roosevelt Papers Vol. 3, p. 234

President Mandates Criminal Sentences Using Interstate Commerce Clause

Criminal legislation based on the interstate commerce clause, the tax clause, and the implied right of the federal government to protect its various agencies and instrumentalities.

Note: 1. Amendments to the federal kidnapping statute to provide for the death penalty in the event of injury to the victim, and creating a presumption that, if the victim was not returned within seven days, the victim had been taken from one state to another.

2. An act punishing the transmission of extortion threats in any form of interstate communications. Prior to this, only the mailing of extortion notes was punishable.

3. A statute making it a Federal offense for a person to flee from one state to another to avoid prosecution for certain major felonies or to avoid testifying in felony cases. Since the enactment of this statute hundreds of persons not available to interstate rendition proceedings have been returned to states under Federal warrants for prosecution.

4. A statute punishing the transportation and receipt of stolen goods in interstate commerce where the value is $5,000 or more. This statute has been instrumental in breaking up some of the larger gangs which had been engaged in shipping stolen merchandise from one state to another.

5. An act punishing robbery of national banks with death penalty where any person is killed during the robbery. The statute is applicable not only to national banks, but to members of the Federal Reserve System and to all banks whose funds are insured by the Federal Deposit Insurance Corporation. It has done much to reduce the epidemic of bank robbery.

President Requires Gun Registration

6. A statute requiring registration of all machine-guns and sawed - off shotguns and rifles.

Other Acts Affecting Criminal Prosecution

7. An act making it a Federal offense to assault or kill Federal officers.

8. An act authorizing agents of the Department of Justice to carry firearms.

9. An act to protect certain types of trade and commerce against intimidation and racketeering.

10. Various statutes for improving the outworn and archaic Federal criminal procedure to make the prosecution of crime in court more effective.

11. A statute granting congressional consent to any two or more states to enter into agreements or compacts for the prevention of crime and the enforcement of criminal laws. As a result of this statute and of the impetus given by the Attorney General, compact statutes have been enacted among many states covering such things as: fresh pursuit compacts (enacted in 21 states) permitting the police of one state to pursue and capture a fugitive across the boundary lines of another state; a simplified uniform extradition procedure providing for quick return of criminals (enacted by compacts in 16 states); return of important witnesses in criminal proceedings from one state to another (adopted by reciprocal laws in 21 states); arrangements for supervising parolees of other states (adopted in 17 states).

Roosevelt Papers Vol. 3, p. 243-244

Statement on Signing Bill to Give the Supreme Court Power to Regulate Procedure in the Federal Courts. June l9, 1934. Roosevelt Papers Vol. 3, p. 303

Presidential Agency Buys Land; Never Returned to Private Ownership

The President asks the congress for additional funds to carry on drought relief. June 9, 1934.

NOTE: As a result of this message, the congress, in full cooperation, voted $525,000,000 to be allocated among the various agencies engaged in drought relief measures.

Roosevelt Papers Vol. 3, p. 294

The Federal Emergency Relief Administration was authorized to purchase lands in stricken areas. Cattle worth $9,815,000 were destroyed. These purchased lands exist today as the public held lands and have not been returned to private lands.

Government Decrees Use of Public Lands

Statement on Signing Bill for Federal Regulation of Grazing on Public Lands. June 26, 1934.

Roosevelt Papers Vol. 3, p. 308

This bill provided that 142 million acres of public land acquired by the government could be grazed.

Executive Order 6766. June 29, 1934 - Protection and conservation of wildlife by providing suitable refuges.

Executive Order 6777. June 20, 1934 - The National Resources Board is established.

The function of the Board shall be to prepare and present to the President a program and plan of procedure dealing with the physical, social, governmental, and economic aspects of public policies for the development and use of land, water, and other national resources, and such related subjects as may from time to time be referred to it by the President.

Roosevelt Papers Vol. 3, p. 335

Government Calls in Silver

Executive Order 6814. Aug. 9, 1934

Requires the delivery of all silver to the United States for coinage.

President Further Tampers with Farm Prices, Imports

Executive Order 2093. August 10, 1934 - allowed importation of duty-exempt feed for livestock in drought areas.

Most favored nation principle. April 5, 1935.
Roosevelt Papers Vol. 4, p. 115

President Controls Utilities

Executive Order No. 7037. May 11, 1935
Establishment of Rural Electrification Administration (R.E.A.)

President Takes Control of Natural Resources

Executive Order No. 7065. June 1, 1935

I hereby prescribe the functions and duties of the National Resources Committee as follows:

(a) To collect, prepare and make available to the President, with recommendations, such plans, data and information as may be helpful to a planned development and use of land, water, and other national resources, and such related subjects as may be referred to it by the President.

(b) To consult and cooperate with agencies of the Federal Government, with the states and municipalities or agencies thereof, and with any public or private planning or research agencies or institutions, in carrying out any of its duties and functions.

(c) To receive and record all proposed Federal projects involving the acquisition of land (including transfer of land jurisdiction) and land research projects, and in an advisory capacity to provide the agencies concerned with such information or data as may be pertinent to the projects. All executive agencies shall notify the National Resources Committee of such projects as they develop, before major field activities are undertaken.

NOTE: The Committee has been cooperating in (1) urban planning, (2) county planning, (3) district planning and (4) state and regional planning.

Roosevelt Papers Vol. 4, p. 243 & 245

Emergency War Control Became Permanent Control; People Forbidden to Sue Government; Government Claims Absolute Immunity

It must be noted that the proceeding are only a small example of the authority exercised by the emergency government. Between the years 1933 and 1936 there were 182 presidential proclamations and 1489 executive orders issued. This does not include the numerous emergency acts passed by congress.

When these powers were permitted to continue on a permanent basis they resulted in a total transformation of the form of government to which the constitutional American system had become long accustomed.

The view of the total power of government can perhaps best be summed up by reading excerpts from "A Message to Congress on Gold Clauses in Government Bonds" written by Roosevelt on June 17, 1935.

To this end, I urge the withdrawal by the United States of its consent to be sued upon its currency or securities.

There is no constitutional or inherent right to sue the Government; on the contrary, the immunity of the sovereign from suit is a principle of universal acceptance, and permission to bring such suits is an act of grace, which, with us, may be granted or withheld by the congress.

Roosevelt Papers Vol. 3, p. 287-288

Government was unrestrained in its prerogative power at least insofar as times of crisis were concerned, and the people were powerless to challenge this sovereign power.

Bitter Opposition Voiced

The view of the opposition, and there was opposition, can best be summed up in the letters sent to Roosevelt by Senator Thomas D. Schall.

> My dear Mr. Roosevelt:
>
> Your telegram to me bears out the suggestion of the constant effort to mislead and fool the public. Your desire to make yourself appear before the people of the United States as a champion of a free press may be as insincere as your promises to the people when you accepted the Democratic nomination at Chicago with the statement that you were for their platform a hundred percent. To date you have not kept one of the covenants you pledged the people at that time. Let me recall your testy anger at your disappointment in keeping out of the press code the expression of a free press.
>
> For me to chronicle all the attempts of your Administration to throttle the press and free speech - all known to you and approved by you in advance - would be but to recite incidents with which you are entirely familiar. If it were not for the fact that I see in your request for "information" an attempt on your part to appear as a victim of your own bureaucracy instead of its chief organizer, I would be inclined to ignore your telegram.
>
> But since you assume a cloak of innocence and since your telegram to me is in the hands of the press, it becomes my duty as a sentinel of the people to do what little I can to mitigate their deception by citing specific evidence of your intention to force a censorship of the press so that your acts and the acts of your communistic bureaucrats might be hidden from public gaze.

I refer as you are quite aware to the statement of your chairman of the Judiciary Committee, Mr. Summers of Texas, in connection with the passage of the press censorship bill by the House in the special session of congress called by you. Under your whip it passed the House and if the Senate had not taken out the poison a publisher who had not gained your approval or the approval of some of your appointees could be sentenced to ten years' imprisonment. The evidence convicting you of a desire to censor the press twenty-five days after you swore to uphold and defend the constitution is in print in the archives of the House of Representatives. Mr. Summers in his statement says the bill was introduced at the request of the "Executive" and is necessary to the success of the recovery legislation. Mr. President, in my opinion, secrecy and press censorship are never necessary when motives are pure.

Every Government department under you is now cloaked in censorship. Almost every bill that has been forced through congress by you has been in itself a little censorship, a little dictatorship either giving blanket powers to you or to some of your left or right hand bowers. According to Garrett you usurped in the extra session of congress 11 powers belonging, under the constitution, to the Judiciary and Congress and when the next congress met you asked that these powers be made permanent. How many powers you have taken from congress and the Judiciary in this last session I have not been able to gather specifically as yet, but they are many. YOU have created some forty-seven bureaucracies. These bureaucracies are clothed with power to make their regulations law. These regulations cover something like 2,000 pages of dictatorship laws made by your appointees of whom not more than one percent has had the sanction of congress.

Your Secretary of the Treasury has two billions of the people's money which he is expending under the protection of a press censorship which you demanded and approved.

You demanded and sanctioned passage of a bill permitting you to secretly fix tariff rates and clothe your acts with a press censorship second to nothing ever before even suggested in the legislative annals of the United States, and this, too, contrary to your Democratic Party platform and contrary to your former specific, vigorous and forceful denunciation of such.

The Communications bill originally introduced by you contained a press censorship clause which was stricken out before the bill was passed but it still gives you the power to inaugurate a Government telegraphic news service, under which as one example you immediately put out of business the three radio stations of Mr. Ford.

You ask me for "information" concerning what you yourself have done. Are you attempting to secure the facts so that you may be in a position to refute yourself?

Yours truly,
Thos. D. Schall

My dear Mr. President:

Your second open telegram to me in no wise explains the various attempts of your Administration to secure legislation censoring the press of the United States.

You requested evidence from me concerning your own acts. I cited you three instances of your efforts to keep the public from securing, through the press, facts concerning the attempts of your bureaucracy to communize the United States.

You say you are acting in "good faith." Then why not as a starter remove the censorship bars against the press that you have placed in all your departments?

Your conclusion to me that the "incident is closed" will in no way, Mr. President, satisfy the people of their fear of where you are unconstitutionally steering their Republic. As a Representative of the people I dare not under my oath to support and defend the constitution let it rest there. The people of the United States want to know from you why their Republic is being gradually cast aside for a dictatorship.

If you desire specific information as to the basis of my reasonable inference, that the Government is about to coordinate its various and sundry publicity functions into a national press service, you have only to assemble the following "makings" thereof:

The White House daily statements, political and economic, which in piecemeal form, not only determine the policies of the world's greatest bureaucracy, but likewise, the major part of political press publication. The free expression of an independent minority giving the public daily exposures of White House blunders and dangerous experiments is naturally disquieting and therefore must be controlled.

The press code which aims to dominate the publishers in the conduct of their business and your opposition to include therein the freedom of press demanded by the publishers' association of which there should have been no dispute, since it is a part of the constitution and is guaranteed in the Bill of Rights.

The Rayburn Communications Act, controlling radio, telegraph, cable and telephone communication, which the American Newspaper Guild pronounces a menace and the foundation of the worst form of "dictatorship ."

Your control of the business offices of the press by Government investment of $1,000,000,000 in the preferred shares of over 6,000 banks - without the credit support of which the publication of a great daily newspaper, or even a magazine and book publishing enterprise having national circulation, would be a business impossibility.

Your domination of all departments of the bureaucracy, in particular, all bureaus publishing current economic data, by which the great bulk of the data is politically "slanted" and damaging data suppressed, with the evident design to foist upon the public the sundry "bold experiments" of the "New Deal." In short it seems to me your Administration's intent is evident and it has become in lock, stock and barrel simply a group of publicity machinery not yet assembled for efficient and smooth operation but if the people return to you another spineless congress the defects no doubt will be remedied and "what we fear will have come upon us."

Your Administration has set up its magazine, called *Today* edited by Brain Truster Raymond Moley and financed by Admiral Vincent Astor of the Flagship *Nourmahl*. What is now needed is a day and night national news service that will cover the daily press field.

All dictatorships and most kings and emperors have their official organs. In Germany, President Hitler has created his ministry of publicity with Goebbels at the head. The Russian Soviet has the Tass Agency. Nothing goes out in Italy without Mussolini's sanction. The news service of the Washington Administration might appropriately be called the WHP-- or White House Press --which would function as the official news service of the "New Deal."

In all fairness, Mr. President, you must admit that you have the "makings" all ready at hand. It is too much for me to call the attention of the Nation to the danger threatened and as Patrick Henry well put it, when he was advocating that the Colonies throw off the yoke of George the Third," I know of no way of judging the future but by the past'"

Sincerely yours,

Thos. D. Schall

Roosevelt Papers Vol 3, p. 365-389

Roosevelt the Man

Franklin Delano Roosevelt, the 32nd president of the United States, was one of the most forceful speakers of his time. His "fireside chats" were the first radio broadcasts ever made by a president directly to the people.

He was elected to an unprecedented four terms in the White House, and served from March 4, 1933 to April 12, 1945. He died two months into his fourth term.

Before becoming president he was Assistant Secretary of the Navy under President Wilson and Governor of New York from 1929 to 1931.

His fireside chats and appeal to the common people did much to carry his programs through.

At one point Roosevelt promised that as soon as the war was over, all the war and emergency powers would return to the people, where they rightly belonged. He died before the war ended.

Chapter Seven

Entrenchment of War Powers

"Your president has the most extraordinary powers, doesn't he?" Mr. Law (a foreign diplomat) looked somewhat wistful.

"Only in war-time."

"Then, if I were an ambitious president, I'd keep the country forever at war."

- Dialogue from the novel *Hollywood* by Gore Vidal

The depression still lingered in the late 1930's. Concentration of economic ownership and control increased, either because of or in spite of Roosevelt's intervention in the marketplace. Roosevelt told congress that private power stronger than the state could not be tolerated.

German armies swept through Europe. Japan was trying to colonize China and Korea. Although the United States was officially neutral, President Roosevelt used war powers to supply troops, weapons, and money to the Allies, without advise or consent from congress. These actions made the US under international law enemies to the Axis, and placed the US squarely and irrevocably on the road to war.

After Pearl Harbor was struck on December 7, 1941, President Roosevelt, using war powers, placed 70,000 American citizens of Japanese descent in concentration camps for two years. He seized the assets of Montgomery Ward & Co. for more than nine months over a labor dispute. He seized other plants more directly related to the war effort.

After Roosevelt died in 1945, new president Harry S Truman ordered bombing of Nagasaka and Hiroshima, which ended the war. President Truman, however, saw fit to continue the war powers, supposedly to aid in post-war reconversion. No war was ever fought to conclusion, including this one.

Germany was partitioned into East and West, the Iron Curtain was formed and the "cold" war began.

America - 1938
Roosevelt Fears Strong Private Power

Many credited the National Reconstruction Act (NRA) with speeding the trend of economic power concentration. Roosevelt told Congress that private power stronger than the government was a threat to the liberty of democracy, and that liberty of democracy was also threatened if business did not provide employment and produce and distribute goods to sustain an acceptable standard of living. He told them he was concerned about centralization of financial control over industry, decline of competition, and employment. He asked for an investigation on how to improve antitrust procedures, mergers, interlocking boards, financial controls, patent laws, tax correctives, and the feasibility of establishing a Bureau of Industrial Economics to act on business the same way the Department of Agriculture did on farming.

The president touted his program as a way to keep business free and productive, to turn business back to the democratic competitiveness. He said free enterprise had not yet been tried in this country, but that monopolies had paralyzed free enterprise.

The Temporary National Economic Committee report echoed the conclusions Roosevelt had cited in his request for investigation. The report came when the New Deal was being merged into a war regime.

Roosevelt Usurps Congress' Treaty Powers

Instead of going through treaty procedures, which would have required the approval of the Senate, Roosevelt made agreements with foreign countries on matters not military without the knowledge of congress.

War Begins in Europe

In 1939, Adolf Hitler, who had come to power in 1933, the same year as Roosevelt, had led Germany into dictatorial government, belief in racial supremacy, and invading Czechoslovakia, Austria, and threatening Poland and the Saar region.

Japan colonized Manchuria and Korea and was trying to get more territory from China.

US Claims Neutrality; Prepares for Defense

The United States' official policy was strict neutrality while preparing for its own defense if necessary.

President Roosevelt issued a proclamation of "limited national emergency" on September 8, 1939. The law makes no provision for a "limited emergency," no distinction in degree, but Roosevelt said he intended to use only a few of the war powers. This meant that even though he called it a limited emergency, he was free to use all the war powers. Any restraint would be strictly self-imposed.

His concern seemed to be with public relations, not the fine points of law.

> Roosevelt said "...if one were to issue a Proclamation of National Emergency without any limitation, scare headlines might be justified, because, under that, the Executive could do all kinds of things."

He revived the Council of National Defense in May, 1940, which members he could appoint without congressional clearance. He established the Office of Emergency Management by executive order on May 25, which became an umbrella unit for many other emergency management bodies. It later became the Office of War Mobilization, then the Office of War Mobilization and Reconversion.

US Provides Weapons to Allies

Although officially neutral, Roosevelt traded 50 American destroyers to Great Britain for American defense bases in British territories in the Caribbean. He informed congress of the agreement later.

> The limited Emergency was a creature of Roosevelt's imagination, used to make it seem that he was doing less than he was. He did not want to create any more furor than was necessary. The qualifying adjective had no limiting role. It was purely for public effect. But the finding that the emergency existed opened a whole armory of powers to the commander in chief, far more than Wilson had had.
>
> - Senate Report 93-549

Concern emerged. Critics charged Roosevelt with flouting congress and the American people, as well as breaking international law. His admirers called it a brilliant stroke of daring statesmanship.

Eight months later, Roosevelt proclaimed a condition of unlimited national emergency.

US Soldiers Seize US Factories

When defense workers struck at the the North American Aviation plant in Los Angeles, Roosevelt sent 2,000 American soldiers to seize the factory for two weeks.

Roosevelt asked congress for power to requisition property for the war effort, and was granted it on October 16.

Two more plants were seized, the Federal Shipbuilding and Drydock Company (E.O. 8868 dated August 23, 1941) and Air Associates Incorporated (E.O. 8928, October 30, 1941).

President Sends Troops to Allies

The president sent American troops to take over non-military duties of the Allies, freeing their soldiers to fight. The US Navy patrolled the Canadian and American coasts while Canadian seamen served the British Navy. The US Navy also protected Greenland by agreement with the Danish minister. Congress found out by reading the newspapers.

Roosevelt supplied troops to Dutch Guiana under agreement with The Netherlands. Again, no communication with congress either before or after the occupation.

By supplying troops to nations at war with the Axis powers, the president had taken steps that were tantamount to placing the United States itself at war. Under international law, the United States became enemies to the Axis.

Roosevelt in 1940 made agreements with Columbia, Panama, and Costa Rica that the US could use their airfields to defend the Panama Canal, and leased naval bases in Brazil and Chile.

War Decisions Made at Secret Conference

The Atlantic Conference was held suddenly and secretly, attended by high-ranking military and government officials. The result was the Atlantic Charter, a statement of ideals, without a disclosure of plans for their accomplishment. Several agreements were made but were only revealed much later.

US Protects Monies of Allies, Blacklists Others

The president protected the assets of nations threatened by Axis powers by freezing their assets in the US. On April 10, 1940, he issued E.O. 8389 protecting monies of Norway and Denmark. Later he protected monies of The Netherlands, Belgium, Luxembourg, France, Monaco, Latvia, Lithuania, Estonia, Romania, Bulgaria, Hungary, Yugoslavia, Greece, Albania, Andorra, Austria, Czechoslovakia, Danzig, Finland, Germany, Italy, Liechtenstein, Poland, Portugal, San Marino, Spain, Sweden, Switzerland, and the Union of Soviet Socialist Republics. On July 26, 1941, he added China and Japan to the list.

On July 17, 1941, the president blacklisted 1,800 Latin American firms for aiding Italy or Germany.

President Sends War Materials to Allies, Patrols Seas

The Lend Lease Act of March 11, 1941 gave the president the power to give war materials to nations whose defense the president thought vital to the defense of the US. Defense production escalated.

On April 29 the president announced that he would extend neutrality patrols as far as he deemed necessary. Admiral Stark disclosed that they were already operating 2,000 miles out at sea. After several denials, the president admitted that US convoys were escorting arms to Britain.

All these things were done by the president, using war powers, without advise or consent from congress or the American people.

Pearl Harbor Attack Should Have Been No Surprise

To any American who had the slightest knowledge of international law, the Japanese bombing of Pearl Harbor on December 7, 1941, should have been no surprise. As early as 1933 the president had placed the United States into the position of an ally with Great Britain. Under international law this made the US an enemy to the Axis. They restrained for three years before retaliating.

Congress declared war on Japan the next day after Pearl Harbor, and on Germany and Italy three days later. This was the transition from the New Deal to a war regime.

President Sends 70,000 American Citizens to Concentration Camps

The president, (Executive Order 7066 February 19, 1942), sent American soldiers to oust 70,000 American Citizens of Japanese descent from their homes and put them in concentration camps for two years.

Obviously the constitution remained suspended and martial rule prevailed. The "enemy" was totally controlled; American citizens were rounded up like cattle with no regard to constitutional common law or due process. The Supreme Court supported these actions.

When these Americans were released, they found their homes destroyed or occupied by others and their possessions stolen.

Montgomery Ward & Company Seized for 9 Months

Montgomery Ward & Company was seized in December, 1944, after two years of feuding with the government over wartime labor policies. The government held their assets for nine months.

The Emergency Price Control Act of January 30, 1942, gave the president authority to control most goods and services used by the American people.

Roosevelt Promises Power Will Revert to People

At one point Roosevelt promised "And when the war is won, the powers under which I act will automatically revert to the people of the United States - to the people to whom these powers belong."

Roosevelt Dies; Bombs End War

When FDR died on April 12, 1945, President Harry S Truman took over. A few weeks later he ordered the bombing of Nagasaki and Hiroshima, which ended the fighting but not the executive's war powers.

Americans Win the War but Get Stuck With Bill; Truman Wants War Powers for Reconversion (Marshall Plan)

Truman chose to continue the emergency war powers to deal with post-war reconversion. Parts of the war powers acts passed by congress were extended and parts were incorporated into the First Decontrol Act of 1947 and the Second Decontrol Act of 1947.

There was no longer a need for a declaration of war for the government to exercise dictatorial powers. No war, including World War II, was fought to a conclusion. World War II ended with the partitioning of Europe into the western and eastern blocks. Germany was partitioned into East and West Germany. The Iron Curtain was formed and the "Cold War" declared.

War powers were again reaffirmed in the Emergency Powers Interim Continuation Act approved April 14, 1952. This was done so that the US could provide an international police force to the United Nations.

The Korean War, termed a "police action," ended with an agreement of statements, with North and South Korea continuing as adversaries. Viet Nam and recently Iraq ended in much the same way. Consequently, the US remains in a continuous state of emergency or war.

Truman Shares His Concept of the Constitution

Many years later, at his birthday dinner in 1954, former president Truman shared his views of the Constitution. He said:

"There's never been an office - an executive office - in all the history of the world with the responsibility and the power of the Presidency of the United States. That is the reason in this day and age that it must be run and respected as at no other time in the history of the world because it can mean the welfare of the world or its destruction.

"When the founding fathers outlined the Presidency in Article II of the Constitution, they left a great many details out and vague. I think they relied on the experience of the nation to fill in the outlines. The office of the chief executive has grown with the progress of this great republic. It has responded to the many demands that our complex society has made upon the Government. It has given our nation a means of meeting our greatest emergencies. Today, it is one of the most important factors in our leadership of the free world.

"Many adverse elements entered into the creation of the office, springing, as it did, from the parent idea of the separation of powers.

"In the first place, the President became the leader of a political party. The party under his leadership had to be dominant enough to put him in office. This political party leadership was the last thing the Constitution contemplated. The President's election was not intended to be mixed up in the hurly-burly of partisan politics.

"I wish some of the old gentlemen could come back and see how it worked. The people were to choose wise and respected men who would meet in calm seclusion and choose a President and the runner-up would be Vice President.

"All this went by the board - though much of the original language remains in the Constitution. Out of the struggle and tumult of the political arena a new and different President emerged - the man who led a political party to victory and retained in his hand the power of party leadership. That is, he retained it, like the sword of Excalibur, if he could wrest it from the scabbard and wield it."

"And today our Government cannot function properly unless the President is master in his own house and unless the executive departments and agencies of the Government, including the armed forces, are responsible only to the President."

Congress Loses Power to Declare War

War is no longer declared by congress. That power has been permanently delegated to the executive, under the continuing state of emergency. It is because of this permanent war power in the office of the president that he can thrust the US into any international war he chooses.

To this day the US continues to act as the world police for the United Nations. The Korean, Vietnam, Iraq, and Somalia wars were all authorized and fought under the auspices of the United Nations. Not once has congress declared war following the end of World War II.

Recall that President George Bush told congress before the Iraq war that he "would like their support for the U.N. Security Council resolution," but if they failed to support it, he would commit the troops anyway. Bush committed troops to Somalia before congress was even informed.

When President Bill Clinton was inaugurated in 1993, war planes were bombing Iraq. It is clear that a permanent state of emergency existed at least into 1993.

Farm Prices, Controls Regularly Exercised

Farm prices and production continue to be controlled to the extent that many farmers say they have been regulated to mere feudal serfs on the land. A few examples of this emergency war power control over agriculture are as follows:

August 29, 1949 - An Act to Amend the cotton and wheat marketing quota provision of the A. A. A.

August 1, 1972 - Executive Order No. 11677 Continuing the Regulation of Exports

By virtue of the authority vested in the President by the Constitution and statutes of the United States, including Section 5(b) of the act of October 6, 1917, as amended (12 U.S.C. 95a), and in view of the continued existence of the national emergencies declared by Proclamation No. 2914 of December 16, 1950, and Proclamation No. 4074 of August 15, 1971, and the importance of continuing (a) to exercise the necessary vigilance over exports from the standpoint of their significance to the national security of the United States; (b) to further significantly the foreign policy of the United States and to aid in fulfilling its international responsibilities; and (c) to protect the domestic economy from the excessive drain of scarce materials and reduce the serious inflationary impact of abnormal foreign demand, it is hereby ordered:

Section 1. Notwithstanding the expiration of the Export Administration Act of 1969, as amended, the provisions for administration of that act contained in Executive Order 11533 of June 4, 1970 shall continue in full force and effect and shall authorize the exercise and administration of export controls, under the authority vested in me as President of the United States by section 5(b) of the act of October 6, 1917, as amended (12 U.S.C. 95a).

Executive Order No. 11677 p. 719- 720

Congress Debates;
Decides It's OK to Lower Farm Prices

The effects of this executive order can be seen from excerpts from the hearing before the Committee on Banking, Housing, and Urban affairs, United States Senate, 93rd Congress first session on S 2053 - To amend the Export Administration Act of 1969, to permit the president to use export controls to curtail serious inflation in domestic prices. June 25 and 26, 1973.

Mr. Dent. Mr. Chairman, and members of the committee, as you know, on June 13, 1973, President Nixon announced a series of actions which were being taken to stabilize the economy. He stated that he would seek new and more flexible statutory authority needed to impose export controls on commodities, in the event such action is necessary to curtail serious domestic inflation. He also announced the establishment of reporting requirements for exports of agricultural commodities. We are appreciative of the promptness with which this committee scheduled hearings to consider these matters which we know reflects the strong concern of the Senate that appropriate action must be taken promptly to reduce inflation.

A major source of inflation during 1973 has been due to rising farm product prices. Through May of this year, wholesale prices for farm products have risen more than 22 percent to a level of almost two-fifths above that of May 1972. These sharp price increases reflect reduced output of a number of commodities in both domestic and in international markets coupled with expanding demand pushed up by increases in population and income.

In view of the tight supply situation which began developing in late 1972, the Cost of Living Council made a decision in January 1973, to continue mandatory controls in the food sector. At the same time, the Council in cooperation with the U.S. Department of Agriculture took a number of major steps to implement strong policy actions designed to encourage a vigorous expansion in farm output during 1973.

During the opening months of the year, it appeared that the actions to augment farm output and the incentive of rising farm product prices would lead to increased supplies of both crop and livestock production, particularly in the second half of 1973. However, market prices for grains and soybeans have risen sharply in recent weeks and have resulted in upward pressure on livestock prices. This run up in feed costs during the late spring put a severe squeeze on livestock profits and forced many operations into loss positions.

This upsurge in prices during the late spring, coupled with evidence of runaway prices in other commodity markets led to the President's announcement on June 13 that a freeze would be imposed on prices for 60 days. This action was taken to halt inflation immediately and to allow time for the development and implementation of a set of wage and price controls that would take effect on or before August 12 in order to restore reasonable price stability.

With respect to agricultural products and other commodities influenced by international markets, it is becoming increasingly evident that unless the United States takes positive steps to protect its markets, commodities will flow to other countries where consumers with increasing incomes are eating more meat than before and paying higher prices than in the United States..

Senate Hearing - Export Controls p. 4

Senator Proxmire. I want to make sure I understand what the essence of the proposal is. I take it that when you say that the proposal would provide that either a finding of an abnormal foreign demand or that the commodity be controlled as a scarce material would be sufficient to provide for export licensing, or export restraints, is that correct? That is No. 1.

Then No. 2, in addition even if those findings are not relevant or applicable, it would provide that controls can be authorized when necessary to control serious domestic inflation.

That phrase by itself can be applied even if the other two are not appropriate, is that correct?

Mr. Dent. That is correct; yes, sir.

Senate Hearing - Export Controls p. 8-9

Secretary Butz (Secretary of Agriculture). We have had two devaluations of the dollar and a de facto evaluation in the last few weeks, which makes the American market more attractive. But I think you put your finger on our real need for legislation of this kind, and that is to protect the feed supply of the domestic livestock and dairy industry.

Senator Bennett. I appreciate your saying that in so many simple words, because I think this is the basic issue here and I think the President must have the power to keep these grains from flowing out if we are going to have any hope of getting a handle on either the price of meat or the price of poultry.

Senate Hearing - Export Controls p. 13

Senator Stevenson. There are numerous ways in which the Government can intervene in the marketplace to control exports and imports. One way is through devaluation of the dollar, or through revaluation upwards of the dollar.

What, if any, consideration is being given in the Treasury now in view of the de facto devaluation of the dollar to some defense of the dollar through swap arrangements, perhaps borrowing marks and using them to buy dollars or through the sale of gold reserves in the unofficial market?

Senate Hearing - Export Controls p. 19

Secretary Butz. I am basically a market/price economist. I think in our kind of society, price performs a very essential function, and when you try to interfere with it on a massive scale, as we have been doing, not alone in the last couple of years, but I would say progressively over the last 2 or 3 decades, you introduce maladjustments; you introduce uneconomic distribution schemes: you introduce uneconomic cost/price relationships that tend to get frozen in. Then you raise the question of how do you get off that.

One of the things that concerns me greatly is that each time we impose a new set of controls, when we back off, we never back off quite as far as we were before we imposed the controls, and your de-escalation is always on a higher plane each time you de-escalate, and we move further and further away from the kind of economy we have had.

The thing - the chief thing we have to guard against is that we do not destroy the incentive system which has been inherent in the American free enterprise economy. That finds its most powerful expression in profit, and when you set out to regulate profit to de-emphasize profit, to try and get production out of a situation that has inherently frozen into it a disincentive system. I think you are moving essentially away from the free society we have known.

There are two ways - to come back to meat production, for example, - there are two ways that you can encourage added meat production, and that is what we are talking about here, how to get added meat production. The rest of 1973, into 1974, and 1975, we have to recognize that decisions we make in June 1973 have an impact on the supply of beef in June 1975, because there is no way that you can get a 2-year-old steer in much less time than 24 months. It takes about that long to do the process.

If we signal back to producers right now an unfavorable profit situation, they interpret that as a signal that we want less meat, not more. So, you can use the price system as a means of signaling back to them to get more, or in the absence of that, if you move to a totalitarian society as the Soviet economists are, for example, you can make decisions in Washington and allocate resources and assign them and set production quotas, entirely disregarding the profit system.

The interesting thing is, as we sit here,...having had a price-oriented economy, we are the nation's breadbasket. The Soviet nations, having had a controlled economy and having directed resources in the food sectors of their economy, are now the deficit food nations, and they are buying from us.

What bothers me is the very thing that you have just indicated, and that is that we are moving more toward their system as they move more towards ours. Ours has the record of success. Theirs has the record of failure.

Senate Hearing - Export Controls p. 24-25

Secretary Butz. We are pulling some 25 to 43 million acres back into production this year that were not utilized last year. We are not quite at capacity this year, but the acres not being used this year are marginal acres.

Next year I would anticipate we will be in full production.

Senator Hathaway. With regard to Senator Johnston's questions, you commented that you didn't care much for administered prices, as I understand it?

Secretary Butz. That is a personal opinion of mine.

Senator Hathaway. Given the noncompetitive society we have, administered prices is the only solution with giant industries -

Secretary Butz. We are becoming closer and closer and closer to it on many fronts, there are institutional prices. We have it in the labor front, of course, with institutional prices. We have it in the cost of money which is virtually institutional pricing. I guess we are moving toward it in agriculture. I am being dragged in myself by my heels.

Senator Hathaway. We don't have much choice in agriculture, do we?

Senate Hearing - Export Controls p. 32

Senator Proxmire. I wonder if the Senator would feel the same way if the election had been reversed and Senator McGovern would have been the elected leader?

Senator Bennett. The problem would have been there; I think we would have had to give President McGovern the tools.

Mr. Walker. I would like to make an observation that Dr. Dunlop made, that when this relates to exports and possible shortages in the commodities in the domestic market, then there is some anticipatory inflationary effect of having public protracted discourse on the suitability of whether or not export controls ought not be imposed: therefore it is our feeling that export controls to curtail serious domestic inflation is the last remaining tool that the President lacks at the present time to deal with the problem. And that - for that reason, standby authority ought to be granted him for future use promptly when shortages show up and increased excessive rates, shall we say, of exports which appear on commodities where there is a short supply here, and where it would help curtail domestic inflationary crisis by restricting imports.

Senate Hearing - Export Controls p. 34-35

Dr. Johnson. If there is a major grain crop failure anywhere in the world - or even rumors of such a failure - it is highly probable that the rise in international prices for one or more major grains would result in increased U.S. exports and an increase in domestic prices above current levels.

Such crop failures - or rumors of them - cannot be ruled out. Given the domestic price controls, I believe that the President should have the authority to limit exports to a level consistent with grain and feed prices no higher than those now prevailing.

Senate Hearing - Export Controls p. 38

Dr. Johnson. Export controls were imposed on cotton in 1950 following a poor crop in the United States and a sharp rise in market prices. The average price received by farmers for the 1949 crop of cotton was 28.6 cents per pound; for the 1950 crop the price was 40.1 cents, even with the export controls. But the price would surely have gone much higher without the export controls. Prices of reasonably comparable foreign growths increased by 80 percent between the 2 years while the domestic price increased by 40 percent.

The 1950-51 experience with export controls illustrates a problem that I feel should be recognized. If export controls are imposed and the controls are effective in limiting exports, the value or price of a product will be greater than the domestic price. Thus someone will enjoy a windfall and I assume that the gain will go to the foreign importing agency.

The only way to prevent this is to impose an export tax or its equivalent. I know the U.S. Constitution does not permit the imposition of an export tax, but Congress was ingenious enough to devise wheat export marketing certificates, Public Law 88 -297, April 11, 1964. As with the wheat export marketing certificates, any amount collected could be distributed to producers. I assume the distribution of the receipts from the wheat export marketing certificates to farmers was the basis for not classifying the certificates as an export tax.

I will conclude with two brief comments: First, I have considerable experience in the design and administration of price ceilings for agricultural products - particularly livestock products - as an employee or consultant to both OPA and OPS. Thus I speak from a base of experience as well as empirical and theoretical knowledge of the functioning of markets.

Senate Hearing - Export Controls p. 39

Senator Johnston. Without being willing to pay that price, aren't we really asking for permanent controls because sooner or later you either have to face that music or you have to keep the controls on?

Senate Hearing - Export Controls p. 41

John Schnittker. The basic objective of export controls, if applied now, would be to reduce U.S. prices of feed grains and soybeans. Meat price ceilings were imposed prior to the general price freeze announced June 13, based upon meat prices during March, when livestock feed prices were high by previous years standards but far below current levels.

Senate Hearing - Export Controls p. 51

Farm Market Constantly Tweaked

December 23, 1985 Public Law 99 -186 (HR 2100)

An Act to extend and revise agricultural price supports and related programs, Amends the A. A. A and Food Stamp Act of 1977.

November 15, 1990 Public Law 101- 511 (HR 5871)

An Act to amend the farm poundage quota provisions of See. 319 of the A. A. A.

April 10, 1990 Public Law 101- 270 (HR 4099)

Suspends Section 332 of the A. A. A. of 1938 requiring USDA establish a national marketing quota for the 1991 wheat crop.

August 14, 1989 Public Law 101- 62 (HR 2467)

To provide disaster assistance to agriculture producers. Amends A. A. A. to authorize emergency assistance for livestock feed, transportation, and water.

Proclamation No. 5294 January 28, 1985.

A Proclamation

"By Proclamation No. 5071 of June 28, 1983, I imposed, on an emergency basis, import quotas on certain sugars, blended syrups and sugars mixed with other ingredients. These quotas were to be effective pending my further action after receipt of the report and recommendations of the United States International Trade Commission (hereinafter "Commission") on this matter pursuant to Section 22 of the Agricultural Adjustment Act of 1933, as amended (7 U.S.C. 624). (hereafter "Section 22"). The Commission has made its investigation and reported its findings to me."

Control Over Agriculture Continues Today

These examples show conclusively that the Agricultural Adjustment Act of 1933 was enacted to form a permanent state of emergency rule over agriculture, and this emergency rule continues to this day.

Furthermore the Nixon price freezes and the grain embargoes of Nixon, Ford, Carter, Reagan and Bush were seizure actions of war for which the American farmer has never been compensated.

It is due to this lack of compensation and war power policy that hundreds of thousands of family farmers have been systematically eliminated and removed from the land that their grandfathers fought to defend.

It is impossible today for young farmers to purchase land. The price of land is arbitrarily inflated to maintain the securities that back the Federal Reserve Bank Notes. The price of commodities is arbitrarily deflated to supply the consumer with cheap food.

Wheat Price Same as 90 Years Ago

As noted earlier in this report the price of wheat in 1917 was mandated not to drop below $2.00 per bushel. The price of wheat in July of 1992 was $2.30 per bushel. The price has not changed significantly for 90 years. Anyone who realizes this must know that the family farmers are doomed. In the end there will be only one large government farm.

All should visualize the problems of Russia over the past 3 years with this same agricultural system in place. They could not feed themselves today were it not for the remaining remnant of family farms in the United States.

Although we use many examples of control in agriculture, other industries are controlled and manipulated just as heavily.

Everyday Life, Business is Controlled by War Powers

The war and emergency powers affect the everyday lives of Americans, including everything from labor relations to prices.

Senate Polls Agencies on Termination of War Powers

In 1973 the Senate began a study to terminate the continuing national emergency. This Senate Report begins with:

"Since March 9, 1933 the United States has been in a state of declared national emergency."

The Senate asked the departments, agencies, and committees to recommend how emergency and war power statutes should be dealt with; should the national emergency be terminated?

Agencies Recommend Retaining or Broadening War Powers

The agencies responded in general with the recommendation to make the authorities vested by the war powers into permanent legislation, and in some cases even to broaden them. Here are some typical responses:

Committee on Banking, Housing and Urban Affairs
Washington, D.C., August 1, 1974
Hon. Frank Church,
Hon. Charles . Mathias, Jr.,
Cochairmen, Special Committee on the Termination of the National Emergency, U.S. Senate, Washington, D.C.

Dear Senators Church and Mathias:

This is in reply to your request for the recommendation of the Senate Committee on Banking, Housing and Urban Affairs as to whether national emergency statutes under the jurisdiction of this Committee should be repealed, recast as permanent legislation, or amended to meet present circumstances.

A review of the compilation provided by your Special Committee has been accomplished. This Committee's recommendations pursuant thereto are attached in memorandum form.

A nine month grace period between enactment and effect of legislation terminating any state of national emergency should provide sufficient time in which to recast or amend those statutes considered to be of permanent utility.

I trust that this review will prove satisfactory.

With best wishes, I am

Sincerely,

John Sparkman.

Attachment.

LAWS APPLICABLE TO PERIODS OF NATIONAL EMERGENCY

Title 12 Banks and Banking Title 12 U.S.C. 95 and 95a

It is the Committee's recommendation that these sections of Title 12 be retained in their present form.

The executive replied also.

12 U.S.C. 95. Emergency limitations and restrictions on Business of members of Federal Reserve system:

In order to provide for the safer and more effective operation of the national banking system and the Federal reserve system, to preserve for the people the full benefits of the currency provided for by the Congress through the national banking system and the Federal Reserve system, and to relieve interstate commerce of the burdens and obstructions resulting from the receipt on an unsound or unsafe basis of deposits subject to withdrawal by check, during such emergency period as the President of the United States by proclamation may prescribe, no member bank of the Federal Reserve system shall transact any banking business except to such extent and subject to such regulations, limitations,and restrictions as may be prescribed by the Secretary of the Treasury, with the approval of the President. Any individual, partnership, corporation, or association, or any director, officer, or employee thereof, violating any of the provisions of this section shall be deemed guilty of a misdemeanor and, upon conviction thereof, shall be fined not more than $10,000 or, if a natural person, may, in addition to such fine, be imprisoned for a term not exceeding ten years. Each day that any such violation continues shall be deemed a separate offense. (Mar. 9, 1933, ch. 1, title I, 4, 48 Stat. 2.)

Recommendation: The Treasury Department recommends retention of this statute in its present form.

This section should be retained. The Congress may wish to enlarge the scope of the statute to cover all banks and other financial institutions located in the United States, including foreign banks having offices or branches here.

The Federal Reserve Board replied to the Senate inquiry about which war powers to retain: "...we are not aware of any emergency laws still in force which do not appear in the United States Code."

The Federal Reserve Board recommended that the emergency statutes be repealed, because the "Code" will allow them to continue the emergency on a permanent statutory basis.

Although these are only examples of the responses of the many agencies and bureaus, they all answered in much the same way.

In 1976, Congress passed the National Emergency Termination Act, abiding by the recommendations. The termination was in name only; the emergency powers were continued in the U.S. Code as permanent everyday powers.

Section 5(b) of the Act of October 6, 1917 as amended March 9, 1933, the Trading With the Enemy Act, was again expressly exempted from the termination.

This documentation shows that a state of emergency has become a permanent condition. By now it is obvious that should the emergency or war be terminated, the United States must return to its peacetime money; i.e. gold and silver coin.

It is also obvious that the gold, silver, and property that has been seized during this time must also be returned.

America continues under the constitutional dictatorship of war and emergency power to this day. (Title 12 U.S.C. Sec. 95 a and b)

Harry S Truman was a Missouri judge and senator before becoming Vice President. He served the rest of FDR's term upon his death, and was elected president in 1948.

Mr. Truman's middle name was S, therefore there is no period after the letter. Journalists who insisted on using a period were one of his pet peeves.

Chapter Eight

War Powers in Germany, France and England

The rise and fall of the Third Reich is simply a story of the use and abuse of war and emergency powers.

- Eugene Schroder

America was not the only country in economic trouble in the 1930's. The depression was worldwide.

Germany, France, and England all used emergency powers to deal with the economy, but with vastly different results. Each constitution's emergency clause was framed differently, with Germany's being the loosest and France's the most restricted.

Germany's Emergency Power Clause Allows Hitler to Become Dictator

Article 48 states:

If a state does not fulfill the duties incumbent upon it under the national Constitution or laws, the President of the Reich may compel it to do so with the aid of the armed forces.

If the public safety and order in the German Reich are seriously disturbed or endangered, the President of the Reich may take the measures necessary to the restoration of the public safety and order, and may if necessary intervene with the armed forces. To this end he may temporarily suspend in whole or in part the fundamental rights established in Articles 114 (inviolability of person), 115 (inviolability of domicile) 117 (secrecy of communication), 118 (freedom of opinion and expression thereof), 123 (freedom of assembly), 124 (freedom of association), and 153 (inviolability of property).

The President of the Reich must immediately inform the Reichstag of all measures taken in conformity with sections 1 or 2 of this Article. The measures are to be revoked upon the demand of the Reichstag.

A national law shall prescribe the details.

Germany existed under the Weimar Constitution from 1919-1933. The "dictatorship article" in its constitution, Article 48, allowed Hitler to suspend the constitution.

The president and his cabinet were allowed to determine what were "necessary measures" or a serious disturbance of "the public safety and order in the German Reich."

Article 48 became the foundation of Hitler's dictatorship. It was an inexhaustible reservoir of emergency power.

The life and death of the Weimar Constitution is simply a story of the use and abuse of Article 48, which itself was patterned in the Western tradition.

Germany's president used Article 48 in 1922 to deal with an economic crisis. By executive decree, speculation in foreign currency was forbidden. This was the first time the president's emergency powers were used to deal with an economic situation. President Ebert and Chancellor Wirth had determined that "the public safety and order" could be "seriously disturbed and endangered" by economic upheaval. Emergency economic decrees were regarded as "necessary measures."

Paul von Hindenburg became the second president of the Reich in 1925. He used Article 48 only to revoke decrees issued by Ebert. From 1925 to 1929 Germany enjoyed its only years of political and economic well-being.

In the severe crisis of 1930-1933, the cabinet enforced a strenuous economic dictatorship on the basis of Article 48. The cabinet found their legal basis in a series of enabling acts authorizing the executive to issue executive orders having the force of regular law.

Chancellor Heinrich Bruning of the Center Party was asked to form a new cabinet. He proposed tax increases to take care of declining receipts and mounting expenses. When the Reichstag rejected them, Bruning implemented them by executive order using Article 48. When the Reichstag demanded revocation, Bruning dissolved both the decrees and the Reichstag, re-issuing his orders a few days later.

Although Bruning was trying to save Germany from financial collapse, his actions paved the way for Hitler's dictatorship in the future.

The Reichstag elections dealt a staggering blow to the cause of freedom. The Nazis increased their seats from 12 to 107 and the Communists from 54 to 77. Both were sworn enemies of the Republic.

The largest party, Social Democrats united behind Bruning to swing a vote of confidence of 318-236, but then adjourned. The Social Democrats were willing to support Bruning as chancellor but not to cooperate with him in enacting his drastic emergency programs.

This Reichstag sat only six times during its 20-month existence, and passed only two laws. Over one third of its members were openly trying to destroy the system. The Reichstag could not function under such conditions.

Bruning had no choice but to assume the entire legislative function. Article 48 was used as the basis to legislate finances, taxes, customs, justice, governmental organization and commerce after the Reichstag abdicated their duties.

Much of Roosevelt's "New Deal" legislation was copied after Bruning's attempts to save the German republic from financial collapse. However, Bruning had no sitting congress, and Roosevelt did.

Adolf Hitler took office on January 30, 1933, the same year as Roosevelt. The Reichstag was dissolved, and Hitler issued his first set of executive orders based on Article 48.

The new Reichstag then passed an enabling act giving Hitler full powers of executive decree. Hitler scrapped the constitution for good. The Weimar Constitution, with its Article 48 had become a bridge to despotism, and over this bridge marched Adolf Hitler. Germany's grisly history after Hitler is well known.

France's Emergency Powers Well Defined, Set to Expire Automatically

France, on the other hand, had laid out the terms and conditions of its emergency war powers, or state of siege, as they called it, very specifically and methodically.

France's state of siege can only be declared by a law, and this law designates the application and duration. On its expiration date, it ceases automatically unless a new law is passed. The end of the state of siege brings a virtually complete return to normal government and civil life.

The French president can only declare the state of siege if the chambers are adjourned. Otherwise, the chambers must declare the state of siege.

The 1930's brought the same economic turmoil and depression to France as it had to Germany. As a result, in 1935, an enabling act was passed allowing the government until August 31, 1937, "to issue decrees having the force of law designed to prevent speculation and to defend the franc." The Laval government turned out more than 500 decree laws that summer which played havoc with private obligations. Public pensions and salaries were lowered, interest on government securities was lowered, rents and utility rates were fixed, and the entire economy was regulated. In 1937 the franc was devalued, taxes were raised, and exchange controls were established.

A new law in 1938 gave even more power to the Daladier cabinet, which enacted a set of laws dealing with public utilities regulations, reform of local finances, control of transportation, custom duties, housing, agriculture, and the entire defense effort. The government mobilized all laborers and requisitioned the railroads.

In 1940 during the Nazi occupation, Constitutional Act No. 2 gave the Petain government the uncontrolled power to declare the state of siege in all of France.

Great Britain Hands Full Power to Churchill; Parliament Continues to Air Issues

Great Britain had anticipated necessity of constitutional dictatorship in much the same way France had.

During the 1930's, Great Britain also had an unbalanced budget, severe unemployment, depreciation of security values, industrial stagnation, and a weakening of the entire financial structure. Parliament passed five statutes giving Ramsay MacDonald temporary powers of executive lawmaking.

The MacDonald "National Government" had its share of constitutional innovations, which apologists say were necessary for mastering the economic crisis.

With the advent of World war II, the British Government had clear title to the powers of constitutional dictatorship. Although Winston Churchill was handed the entire scope of emergency powers, he handled them in a restrained and democratic manner.

The declaration of war caused a basic reorganization of the cabinet and ministry. Some ministers' powers shrank, others expanded. More than 20 new agencies were established. The war cabinet did its work through committees directly responsible to it. As a legislative body, the House of Commons lost most of its peacetime functions. Its membership was frozen for the duration of the war. General elections were postponed repeatedly.

The House of Commons was given the chance to debate and vote upon such vital subjects as conscription, taxation, appropriations, and normal social legislation, but nine times out of ten a bill prepared in one of the ministries went through all the parliamentary stages quickly and without amendment. Even at that, every burning issue was thoroughly thrashed out on the floor of the House. Blockades, air-raid shelters, propaganda, civil liberties, war crimes, and reconstruction were all aired in the open. Secret sessions were held as well. It was generally agreed that this was sometimes necessary to keep secrets out of enemy hands.

One of the most impressive features of the British emergency government was with regard to the civil liberties of the people. Although the freedom of the subject was placed squarely in the hands of the government to respect or invade according to the necessities of the moment, the encroachments were in fact rather trifling.

The Emergency Powers (Defense) Act came to an automatic end February 24, 1946.

Winston Churchill led England through an almost unendurable war.

While addressing a group at Westminster College in Fulton, Missouri in 1946, he coined the term "iron curtain."

Chapter Nine

States Rights Feud Becomes War

Until the Civil War, the federal government was still considered an agent of the states. The Civil War marked a shift in power. The roles were reversed, and the states became subordinate to the federal government. The states rights versus federal rights issue came to a head over slavery.

At the turn of the century, most Americans in both north and south thought that slavery would die out of its own accord. It had already died out in the North because it simply didn't pay.

Southern anti-slavery societies outnumbered northern groups in 1827. Many prominent southerners emancipated their slaves. The Virginia legislature in 1832 debated a proposal for gradual phaseout with compensation for the owners, to be in effect by 1861.

As northerners verbally attacked, southerners became defensive and set out to prove that slavery was not evil but a positive good. Radical voices on both sides became the only ones heard.

Cotton Gin Gives Boost to Slavery

In 1793 Eli Whitney had invented the cotton gin which separated the cotton seed from the fiber. This gave the short-staple cotton the south could grow so well a market in the northern textile mills and throughout the world. Southerners switched from growing tobacco, rice and indigo to cotton.

In 1800 the US had exported $5 million worth of cotton, or 7% of the nation's total exports. By 1860 cotton exports had grown to $191 million and were 57% of the total value of all American exports.

Nearly 4 million slaves worked those southern cotton fields. Yet of 6 million southern whites, only 37,662 owned twenty or more slaves. Only 347,525 owned slaves at all. Most southerners were poor dirt farmers living in poverty. Plantation living was a lifestyle of the rich, not the typical southerner.

Northerners who insisted that slavery be outlawed did not have a plan to accomplish it that would not devastate the southern economy. Northerners were loudly decrying slavery while spinning the cotton into commercial goods in their factories, and northern ships had brought the slaves in the first place. Also, the northern factories used cheap immigrant labor to fuel the industrial revolution. Southerners labeled anti-slavery sentiment as hypocrisy.

North and South Conflict Over Many Issues

Many other conflicts started the antagonism between north and south, but slavery was the issue that made men so angry they did not want to compromise. As attacks mounted, each side closed ranks and became more committed to their position.

The south was an agricultural economy. The north, teeming with immigrants, had built factories and become a manufacturing economy. Northerners began to demand aid and protection from the Federal Government, especially protection from cheap European imports. A strong federal government was necessary to accomplish this.

Southerners, on the other hand, wanted as many cheap imports as they could get, and wanted the national government to keep hands off everything possible.

States Rights Become Vital Issue

James C. Calhoun of South Carolina opposed secession on the grounds that any state could nullify within its borders any act of the federal government which it considered unconstitutional and oppressive. They relied upon states rights for self-protection.

Supreme Court Rules Slavery Protected by Constitution, States Cannot Override

As tension mounted, the Supreme Court played its part. Dred Scott, a slave, sued for his freedom on the grounds that his master had kept him in free states for several years. The court denied it. Chief Justice William Taney delivered the opinion, saying Scott's plea was denied because, first, a slave could not be a citizen of any state and therefore could not sue anyone; and secondly, that the act of congress that forbade slavery in northern states was unconstitutional, and that there was no legal way that slavery could be excluded from any territory.

This decision struck down the Missouri Compromise and the Kansas Nebraska Act which had represented sectional compromise and provided boundaries between free and slave states.

Dred Scott's master freed him voluntarily two months after the Supreme Court had denied his freedom.

At that time Kansas and Nebraska were the battlegrounds of colonization by both north and south. The settlers were to vote on whether to be admitted to the union as either a free state or a slave state. Each side was trying to get a majority of settlers to vote their way. The supreme court ruling meant that this plan was null and void.

In 1858, Abraham Lincoln ran against Stephen A. Douglas for the U.S. Senate. Douglas was the father of the Kansas-Nebraska Act, which the supreme court had just struck down. Pinned in a corner as to how popular sovereignty could co-exist with the Dred Scott decision, Douglas finally said that slavery could not exist without supportive local legislation, that in spite of the supreme court decision, territories were free in the absence of state legislation to the contrary. (This position won Douglas the Senate election, but ultimately won Lincoln the presidency.)

Hostilities Escalate

On May 22, 1856, Senator Preston Brooks caned Senator Charles Sumner into insensibilty on the Senate floor with his gutta percha cane.

The Panic of 1857 left a business depression in the north, but did not affect the south. Northern pressure for higher tariffs and a homestead act (in other words more federal control) mounted. The south dug in on their position of states rights.

John Brown, a northern radical, whom many believed a touch insane, seized the federal arsenal at Harpers Ferry on October 16, 1859. He planned to use the weapons to start a slave insurrection in the south. Although he was swiftly caught and hanged, the south took his actions as the typical northern plan to start rampant bloodshed and pillage throughout the south.

The elections of 1860 took place in this environment. The Republicans nominated Lincoln, who was a moderate on the slavery issue as compared to the other two choices, Seward or Chase. The Republican platform was the north's platform - higher tariffs, railroad subsidies, and homesteading the west.

The south could not unite behind Douglas because some regarded him as a heretic on the slavery issue. The vote split behind Douglas, Breckinridge and Bell. The new Republican party dedicated to eradicating slavery won its first election.

Lincoln Elected on Anti-Slavery, Pro North Platform; South Secedes

The South Carolina legislature had remained in session until the election. On learning its outcome they immediately called a state convention and seceded from the union. Mississippi, Florida, Alabama, Georgia, Louisiana and Texas followed.

On February 8, 1861, delegates from the seceding states met at Montgomery, Alabama and set up a new nation, the Confederate States of America, and a provisional government. Jefferson Davis of Mississippi was elected president. Their new constitution prohibited external slave trade, but enjoined the federal government from passing any law denying the right to own slaves.

Lincoln and Davis both Moderate but Determined

Ironically, Jefferson Davis was also regarded as a moderate. Considering that 600,000 Americans died in the Civil War, we wonder what would have happened if radicals had been in charge!

It is said that the greatest misunderstanding between the north and the south was that neither side realized the other side was desperately earnest. Each side thought they were calling the other's bluff, until the war began and it was too late to turn back.

One southern orator said he would wipe up with his handkerchief all the blood that would be spilled because of secession.

South Attacks Fort Sumter; War Begins

The south attacked Fort Sumter, a union fort on an island near the mouth of Charleston Harbor and the bloody four-year war was on.

Fort Sumter was the visible signal that the war had started, but the war really began when both Lincoln and Davis made up their minds to fight rather than yield.

War Did Not Solve Issue

As with all US wars, this one was not fought to conclusion. States and citizens rights are still a big issue.

Jefferson Davis, elected president of the Confederacy, was born and raised near Lincoln's home in Kentucky. He had been a soldier, congressman, senator, and Secretary of War.

BATTLE FLAG
SEPT. 1861 - APRIL 1865

Chapter Ten

Military Rule Over Civilians

Martial rule, or martial law, is the extension of military rule to the civilian population. All powers of government are taken from civil authority and given to the military. It is an emergency device designed to handle invasion or rebellion.

Nowhere is a better example of martial law found than in its use by the north after the Civil War. The entire south was divided into military districts and ruled by martial law.

South Secedes; Lincoln Takes Emergency Powers

In 1860, following Lincoln's election to the presidency, South Carolina's legislature passed unanimously an ordinance declaring that "the Union now subsisting between South Carolina and the other States, under the name of the United States of America is hereby dissolved."

Seceding on December 20, 1860, South Carolina was followed by Mississippi (January 19, 1861), Louisiana (January 26, 1861), and Texas (February 1, 1861). These states called for a state convention. They framed a constitution and on February 8, 1861, set up a provisional government, giving birth to the Confederate States of America. The Confederate congress immediately gave their chief executive, Jefferson Davis, several specific grants of emergency power.

Lincoln was quoted as saying "If the Union and the government cannot be saved out of this terrible shock of war constitutionally, a Union and a government must be saved unconstitutionally."

The US congress was not in session when this crisis erupted. The first incidence of armed rebellion occurred on April 12, 1861. Lincoln called for a special session to convene July 4. The far-reaching powers that Lincoln assumed in the absence of congress were firmly established by the time congress did meet.

One man and one man only was in control of the US government during the most critical period of its 165 years.

Lincoln Raises Armies, Against Constitutional Law

Lincoln's first step was to issue an executive order declaring that because the seven southern states were forcibly obstructing the execution of the laws of the United States, he was compelled to resort to his constitutional and statutory powers to call forth "the militia of the several states of the union to the aggregate number of 75,000 " to suppress the rebellion and guarantee the execution of the laws. In the same proclamation he called a special session on July 4 "to consider and determine such measures as, in their wisdom, the public safety and interest may seem to demand."

Only congress had the power "to provide for the calling forth the militia to execute the laws of the union." The president became commander in chief only after congress had declared the war and called up the state militias.

Lincoln Blockades Ports, Against Constitutional Law

Before the day Lincoln had set for congress to convene, he blockaded the ports of the south (contrary to both the constitution and the law of nations except when the US was in a declared, foreign war), and ordered 19 vessels added to the Navy. Totally against his constitutional rights he called for volunteers to serve for three years in the army and navy. (The constitution states that congress has the power to raise and support armies.)

Constitutional expert Clinton Rossiter said this of Lincoln's actions: "This amazing disregard for the words of the

Constitution, though considered by many as unavoidable, was considered by nobody as legal."

Lincoln Draws $2 Million from Treasury; Gives to Private Individuals

Lincoln had the Secretary of the Treasury give $2 million dollars of unappropriated US funds to three private citizens of New York who were unauthorized to receive it "to be used by them in meeting such requisitions as should be directly consequent upon the military and naval measures necessary for the defense and support of the Government." (The Constitution says "No money shall be drawn from the Treasury but in consequence of appropriations made by law.")

Lincoln Suspends Writ of Habeas Corpus

The actions of President Lincoln as attempts to maintain public order and to suppress open treason in the loyal sections of the union were even more astounding. The proclamation of April 27 authorized the commanding general of the US Army to "suspend the Writ of Habeas Corpus."

Despite the fact that the Constitution gives this power to congress alone, the president claimed he had the right in case of "necessity."

Lincoln Disregards Ruling of Illegality

Chief Justice Taney in the circuit case of *Ex Parte Merryman* ruled against the president on this action. Lincoln simply disregarded the court.

These actions have been labeled "The Lincoln Dictatorship," an extraordinary eleven weeks of presidential activity unparalleled in the history of the U.S. By the time congress came together on July 4, a complete program of executive, military, legislative and judicial dictatorship was in place.

On July 4 he greeted congress with a "special message," a remarkable state paper in which he described frankly the steps he had taken under the war powers of government and invited whatever ratification congress should think necessary to legalize them.

Congress, faced by Lincoln's irrevocable actions, registered approval. The supreme court, when asked over a year later to determine the legality, held simply this: "that the president of the US has the constitutional power, under such circumstances as he shall deem imperative, to brand as belligerents the inhabitants of any area in general insurrection."

Lincoln issued the official Executive Order #1 on October 20, 1862, establishing a provisional court during the military occupation of Louisiana. (An executive order can only be issued by the commander-in-chief and only has jurisdiction over areas under martial law.)

Constitution Can Be Suspended When President Determines Revolt

In other words, the president has almost unrestrained power to act toward insurrectionary citizens as if they were enemies of the US and thus place them outside the protection of the constitution. This is dictatorial power in the extreme. The constitution can be suspended by any president of the US who ascertains and proclaims a widespread territorial revolt.

Congress Oversteps Its Power

Congress, seemingly wanting to get its share of power, also began to legislate far outside its limits. They formed the Joint Committee on the Conduct of the War, and tried to outdo Lincoln on prosecuting the war. The committee proceeded to question and discipline generals, unseating several of them, making eight volumes of reports, dictating the appointment of Stanton as secretary of war, and fighting with the president over the dismissal of incompetents.

Congress proceeded to exert its will over the southern nation. They passed an act to suppress insurrection, to punish treason and rebellion, to seize and confiscate the property of the rebels, and for other purposes; an act to collect direct taxes in insurrectionary districts; and an act for relief of freedmen and refugees.

All these acts of congress were unconstitutional in times of peace. Seizure actions are prevented by the Fifth Amendment which states "Private property shall not be taken for public use without just compensation." Levy, seizure, forfeiture, sequestration, and captures are purely wartime actions.

Direct taxation of citizens of the states are forbidden to any branch of government. Article I states that taxes shall be apportioned among the several states. Taxation of the citizens is purely a wartime measure. Authority to use this taxing power to provide relief to selected individuals is an act of wartime government prerogatives.

Martial Law Imposed on South

Martial law was imposed across the entire south. Arrest without warrant or indictment, detention without trial, and release without punishment all restricted civil liberty. Lincoln not only suspended the right to indictment by a grand jury, he withdrew the right to a civil trial or even a military trial. Men were imprisoned and released without ever facing a charge in court.

Lincoln suspended publication of several prominent newspapers, took control of the telegraph lines, jailed seditious editors, and denied mailing privileges to their journals. In this way he controlled the flow of public information.

The Supreme Court spoke out against him in the Milligan Case, but the words were a mere protest of his extraordinary powers. What Lincoln did, not what the Supreme Court said, set the precedent for emergency powers.

There is this disturbing fact: Lincoln set a precedent for bad men as well as good. If Lincoln could calmly assert "I conceive that I may, in an emergency, do things on a military ground which cannot constitutionally be done by congress," then some future president, less patriotic, might assert the same thing.

Two Crisis Governments Operating

Two crisis governments arose in this bitter war. The confederacy operated an emergency government similar to the union government.

While one may argue that because Lincoln had a rebellion on his hands, his was a constitutional dictatorship during the Civil War. However, the government over the south after the war under reconstruction was an unconstitutional dictatorship. It was a government of conquest.

Property Confiscated, Taxes Levied

After fighting stopped, emergency power to confiscate the property of those sympathetic to the Confederate States was recognized. Taxes were levied on insurrectionary districts, with special tax commissioners (known as carpetbaggers) appointed by the president. As soon as military authority was established, tax commissioners made assessments on all the lands and lots in the secessionist territory.

These were not ordinary tax sales. The property was seized for trifling taxes and the estates sold. The surplus over and above the amount of tax due was not paid to the owner but turned into the Federal treasury. The customary privilege of redemption was conditional upon the owner taking an oath to support the Constitution of the United States.

The Captured Property Act of 1863 allowed Treasury agents to enter the Confederate States and seize property of a "non-warlike character" after the army swept through. By May 1868, gross sales of property seized under the act was about $30 million dollars, with net value of about $25 million. Almost all the property seized was cotton. The supreme court later ruled that those who would take the oath of loyalty were entitled to have their property returned, but efforts to do so were not especially successful.

Federal Class of Citizens Created

The institution of slavery was also affected by emergency powers of confiscation. Slavery had always been held as a state institution outside federal jurisdiction. In fact, a bitter debate over this issue had almost kept the Declaration of Independence from being ratified. At that time the north compromised and let the southern states keep slavery as a state institution in return for them not walking out of the convention.

With the Civil War, the government seemed to acquire the power to strike down slavery. It was not clearly decided whether this right sprang from rights over belligerents, the international law of nations, or an enlargement of federal municipal police power.

Legislature Overpowers Johnson's Reconstruction; Implements Its Own Crisis Government

After Lincoln's assassination, President Andrew Johnson was left with the task of reconstruction following a plan designed by Lincoln. However, his congress was unwilling to allow Johnson the same powers Lincoln had used. Perhaps this had to do with the fact that Johnson was a southerner from North Carolina.

After a bitter struggle between Johnson and the legislature, the president's mild reconstruction plan was ignored and congress established the act of March 2, 1867 over Johnson's veto. This act implemented a legislative crisis government at a time when there was no rebellion or insurrection.

South Divided Into Military Districts

The act divided the rebel states into military districts and placed them under martial law. Troops were stationed in each district, and people were tried by military tribunals. There were no legal states, and states would not be allowed representation unless they adopted the 14th Amendment to the constitution. The southern districts had no choice: they either ratified the 14th Amendment or became permanent subjects.

Margaret Mitchell in *Gone With the Wind* portrayed the southerners' plight magnificiently.

14th Amendment Sets Several Precedents

The 14th Amendment was important in several ways: (1) It created a new class of federal citizens and these citizens were subject to federal jurisdiction. They would have no protection under the Bill of Rights to the Constitution but could not be denied "due process of law" or equal protection of the laws as defined by federal statutes. (2) The federal government was given police power over the states. Congress was given the power to enforce its will through legislation. (3) No citizen could challenge the validity of the debt incurred while prosecuting the war. (4) The southern people were required to take a loyalty oath to support the federal government and abide by and support all laws and proclamations that had been made during the rebellion.

Under the constitution only public officials were required to take an oath to support the constitution. It was a total reversal of the roles of the people and the government, as well as a reversal of the roles of the state and federal governments.

This resulted in a new form of dictatorship - legislative dictatorship.

It is critical to note that these reconstruction amendments were war amendments, passed in time of crisis government, by crisis governments, and for the benefit of expanded powers of government. The applicability of these amendments to peacetime constitutional government is questionable. However, once power is gained, it is seldom given up.

Abraham Lincoln came from a poor family with no formal education. He became a popular country lawyer, Illinois legislator, and congressman. In 1858 he won a Senate seat after debating Stephen A. Douglas.

His renunciation of slavery made him attractive to the new Republican Party in 1860. He was elected President, conducted the Civil War, freed the slaves, and was assassinated.

He is known as the "Great Emancipator."

Chapter Eleven

War Powers From 1913 to 1932

President Wilson Asks for Specific Powers

President Woodrow Wilson used war powers during World War I, beginning in 1913 with the implementation of the Federal Reserve. Wilson's rule differed from either Lincoln's or Roosevelt's in that his powers came from legislation passed by a congress. Wilson chose to demand express legislative authority for almost every unusual step he felt he had to take.

Wilson achieved his powers by providing strong leadership to the congress and by forthrightly asking for laws giving him the powers he felt he needed. Congress did not give up any of its normal lawmaking powers, and all war statutes were subjected to congressional rigors, some bills being changed considerably before enactment.

Congress Has Unlimited Freedom to Act

Congress now had the power to delegate its power, which is forbidden under the constitutional separation of legislative, executive and judicial powers. Congress enjoyed unlimited freedom to act in areas where it could not delegate its power, again forbidden by the 10th amendment.

The necessity that seems to arise in all modern wars for strict governmental control of production, supply, and transportation was for the first time brought home to the American people during Wilson's administration.

Congress passed enabling acts empowering Wilson to take over and operate the railroads and water systems, shipbuilding facilities, regulate exports, raise an army, and operate the telephone and telegraph systems.

Lever Act Allows President to Control All Necessities

The Lever Act of August 10, 1917 was the largest single delegation of power. It allowed the president to control all "necessaries", requisition foods, fuels and anything else needed for national defense. He could regulate the price of wheat, could operate factories, mines, packing houses, pipelines, fix the price of coal and coke, and could forbid the use of food materials to manufacture liquor.

Wilson had more power than had ever been given to a president at that time. For the first time, a president directed the activities of the nation's economy. Wilson created several agencies under his administrative control: the War Industries Board headed by Bernard Baruch, the Fuel Administration headed by Harry A. Garfield, and the Food Administration headed by Herbert Hoover. Franklin Delano Roosevelt was Wilson's Assistant Secretary of the Navy.

Industry compliance was ensured by licensing, priority regulations, price-fixing, and voluntary cooperation. Appeals to patriotism, publicity, threats of higher taxes, and sometimes coercion were used.

Wilson said "This is a war of resources no less than of men" as he formally took over the railroads on December 26, 1917.

World War I ended with the Armistice of November 11, 1918. Many of the procedures and agencies were disbanded at this time.

Trading with Enemy Act Retained after War

The Trading With the Enemy Act (passed October 6, 1917) was retained. In only a few years it would become of paramount importance. This act probably allowed the greatest transformation of peacetime constitutional government into a permanent constitutional dictatorship ever recorded.

Military Used to Squash Disturbances

Wilson became preoccupied with the League of Nations and left the remaining war powers to his secretary of war. He in turn left decisions to his commanding officers as to when to use troops to put down domestic disturbances. US troops were used on disturbances in Washington D.C. in July, 1919, in Omaha, Nebraska, and in Gary, Indiana. Reasons for arrest, length of detention, and severity of restrictions on the general population were all left to the officer in charge.

War Power over Currency Used as Political Tool

Wilson was replaced by Calvin Coolidge as president. His reign was marked by economic booms in the east and busts in the south and west as a result of using the war power over currency as a political tool. Eventually credit was eased and speculation ran rampant. The roaring twenties were on.

President Coolidge in his last State of the Union address in 1928 said:

"No congress of the United States ever assembled, on surveying the state of the Union, has met with a more pleasing prospect than that which appears at the present time. In the domestic field there is tranquillity and contentment, harmonious relations between management and wage earner, freedom from industrial strife, and the highest record of years of prosperity. In the foreign field there is peace, the good will which comes from mutual understanding, and the knowledge that the problems which a short time ago appeared so ominous are yielding to the touch of manifest friendship. The great wealth created by our enterprise and industry, and saved by our economy, has had the widest distribution among our own people, and has gone out in a steady stream to serve the charity and the business of the world. The requirements of existence have passed beyond the standard of necessity into the region of luxury. Enlarging production is consumed by an increasing demand at home and an expanding commerce abroad. The country can anticipate the future with optimism."

This vision was soon to be replaced with a nightmare.

Stock Market Jumpy

President Herbert Hoover's first problem after inauguration in 1929 was a nervous stock market. Stock prices rose, and so did the volume of speculation. The stock gambler could buy on margin, but when his margin shrunk by falling prices, he was automatically sold out. The system built on a house of cards collapsed on Black Thursday, October 24, 1929.

President Herbert Hoover was also faced with thousands of needy veterans who flocked to Washington D.C. and demanded payment of the soldier's bonus. The House passed the bill approving funds, but Hoover said he would not approve it. The legislation failed, and the congress, at Hoover's urging, appropriated $100,000 to transport the veterans home, then adjourned. Some 11,000 veterans stayed behind during the summer of 1932, located at 24 separate camps in D.C.

General MacArthur Leads Troops Against Veterans

Federal troops, a tank platoon and a cavalry squadron, all led by General Douglas MacArthur, advanced on the Pennsylvania Avenue encampment of veterans on July 28 after disturbances around the federal buildings and a brief riot. Troops drove the veterans toward another encampment at Anacostia and completely destroyed it. Homeless, penniless, and unwanted, the veterans fled, saddened that

US soldiers had attacked them in their own country, a country they had fought to defend.

This was a notable use of war powers based on the government's decision that the veterans endangered public safety.

President Woodrow Wilson had an unprecedent amount of power over the American people and economy during World War I, but he insisted on legislation specifically granting him those powers.

President Calvin Coolidge was buoyant in his State of the Union Address in 1928, saying "This country can regard the present with satisfaction and anticipate the future with optimism."

President Herbert Hoover took the rap for the Great Depression since it began on his watch.

Chapter Twelve

Emergencies Proliferate Under Recent Presidents

But we can no longer risk emergency improvisation of national defense. We have been compelled to create a permanent armaments industry of vast proportions ...

In the councils of government, we must guard against the acquisition of unwarranted influence, whether sought or unsought, by the military-industrial complex. The potential for the disastrous rise of misplaced power exists and will persist.

We must never let the weight of this combination endanger our liberties or democratic processes. We should take nothing for granted. Only an alert and knowledgeable citizenry can compel the proper meshing of the huge industrial and military machinery of defense with our peaceful methods and goals, so that security and liberty may prosper together. - Dwight D. Eisenhower in his farewell address January 17, 1961.

Almost every president since Roosevelt and Truman has used emergency powers extensively, both to send troops to foreign countries and to control domestic production, wages and prices.

Cold War Begins

After World War II, Roosevelt, Stalin and Churchill met at the Yalta Conference. Soviet occupation of Eastern European countries was exchanged for a pledge to allow democratic governments to rise within them. Berlin was divided.

Americans became convinced that the Soviets were trying to communize all of western Europe, as well as Turkey and Greece. In February, 1946, Stalin said in Moscow that there could never be a lasting peace with capitalism. Then Churchill warned of the "iron curtain" that had descended across the middle of Europe.

The cold war had begun.

Truman Says US Must Protect World from Communism

Truman announced the "Truman Doctrine" which said that: "It must be the policy of the United States to support free peoples who are resisting attempted subjugation by armed minorities or by outside pressures."

The Marshall Plan was approved by congress in April, 1948. It sent $12 billion to help Europe rebuild, in the belief that this would help fend off communism.

Thus, once again, the US won the war but got stuck with the bill.

The US followed a policy of containment - building "situations of strength" around the Soviet Union to prevent the spread of communism outward.

America's leaders came to regard the peace of the whole world as the responsibility of the United States. Americans seemed to believe that because their cause was just, whatever they did in its name was right.

Soviet spy rings were discovered in the US, Canada, and Great Britain, fueling fear of communism. Alger Hiss, a former state department official, was convicted of passing secrets to the Soviets. In 1950 a spy ring was uncovered in the Los Alamos atomic plant.

Joseph R. McCarthy's claims of communist conspiracies in the federal government (1950) launched a four-year national crisis.

The Korean War

After World War II, North Korea was under communist control, allied with the USSR and Communist China. South

Korea was supervised by the US Small military advisory units occupied both sides.

After Secretary of State Dean Acheson made a speech on January 12, 1950 saying the US would not protect South Korea, North Korea invaded South Korea.

Truman conferred with Acheson and decided the USSR had directed the invasion.

On June 27, 1950, with no congressional declaration of war, Truman, on his own initiative, committed US military supplies to South Korea, moved the US Seventh Fleet into Formosa Strait, and directed General Douglas MacArthur to send his ground, air, and naval forces against the North Koreans.

In July, the UN Security Council asked that all member states wishing to aid South Korea make military forces available to the United States. With this, Truman became the executive agent for the UN in the Korean war, and MacArthur became the commander in chief.

The US supplied most of the air and sea power and about half of the ground forces, with South Korea supplying most of the rest.

The undeclared war lasted three years and ended in a military stalemate, with North and South Korea still divided. South Korea's leader, Synghman Rhee, was not satisfied with terms of the negotiation, so the US promised him long-term economic aid and expansion of the South Korean army. On July 27, 1953 an armistice was signed, *without the participation of South Korea,* and shooting stopped.

Total death toll was in the millions, with 23,300 Americans killed. In addition, over 40% of the industry and a third of the homes in Korea were destroyed.

The war did not solve anything either militarily or politically, but instead intensified bitterness between North Korea and South Korea,

Containment Policy Now Includes Sending Troops

This war added a new definition to the policy of containment. Containment now included sending Americans to fight, as well as providing money and military aid. This new definition of containment helped lead us into in the 1960s.

Eisenhower Declines Involvement in Several Wars

Dwight D. Eisenhower, president from 1953 to 1961, did not institute any bold new programs, opposed any major expansion in the functions of federal government, but did not repeal established programs. Thus, by default, he helped institutionalize the changes made by Roosevelt and Truman.

Eisenhower was basically a pacifist, despite his military background. He concluded the Korean truce in 1953 and ended the war without victory.

In 1954 he refused to commit troops to help the French in their losing battle in Indochina. He met with Soviet leader Nikita Khrushchev and defused tensions with the USSR for a time.

Eisenhower declined to send troops to support the Hungarian Revolution in 1956, and was instrumental in a cease-fire in the Suez Canal zone.

Under his regime, however, the CIA began to plot against Cuban dictator Fidel Castro, and formulated the plan for the Bay of Pigs invasion. They secretly established anti-communist regimes in Iran and Guatemala, and tried to do the same in Laos and Indonesia.

The Eisenhower administration finalized a treaty with the Nationalist Chinese government on Taiwan, and established the Southeast Asia Treaty Organization (SEATO).

US troops were sent to Lebanon but came home three months later without bloodshed.

When the Soviets shot down an American U-2 spy plane and captured its pilot, Eisenhower took full responsibility for the espionage. The Soviets vented their anger loudly.

By the time he left office, the cold war had heated up. Eisenhower was also criticized for the sluggish economy. Since he had begun no new wars, the frenzy of war production and spending was absent.

Dwight D. Eisenhower, president from 1953 to 1961, was basically a pacifist. He declined several opportunities to involve the US in foreign wars.

The Kennedy Years

President John F. Kennedy, president from 1961 to 1963 when he was assassinated, led the country in a burst of idealism and nationalism. He involved young people in his Peace Corps, and began the Alliance for Progress to boost Latin American nations' economies.

He proposed and implemented the biggest tariff cuts in modern history, and challenged Americans to put a man on the moon.

Bay of Pigs Invasion

Three months into his term, however, Kennedy allowed the CIA Bay of Pigs plan formulated under Eisenhower to proceed. US troops tried to invade Fidel Castro's communist Cuba, but were smashed on the beach, the Bay of Pigs.

Cuban Missile Crisis

In 1962 he discovered the Soviets were moving missiles to launching sites in Cuba. He surrounded Cuba with a blockade and issued a public ultimatum. The Soviets backed down, and the US agreed not to attack Cuba.

The Cuban Missile Crisis was said to have effectively ended the Cold War.

Kennedy introduced reform legislation in health care, education, housing and community development, civil rights, and transportation. He did not have the influence necessary to get the congress to pass most of his measures. However most of his programs were carried out by his successor, Lyndon B. Johnson. These included the War on Poverty, the domestic Peace Corps VISTA, and Medicare.

Kennedy sent 16,000 military advisors and ammunition in response to an internal revolution that threatened to destroy South Vietnam.

Kennedy was assassinated on November 22, 1963, shocking the world. The psychological links he had forged between young people and "the system" went by the wayside.

John F. Kennedy, a charismatic president who united young and old in a new feeling of patriotism and striving for excellence, was cut down only two years into his term. Results of the investigation of his assassination have never been fully accepted.

Lyndon Johnson Escalates Vietnam War

The French had fought against North Vietnam since 1947. The US backed their efforts so that by 1953 the US was providing 80% of the costs of France's war. In 1954 France withdrew after being essentially defeated, and appealed to the Geneva Conference. Vietnam was divided into communist North and pro-western South by the Geneva Conference. Neither the United States nor South Vietnam signed the agreement.

Eisenhower's SEATO provided for US intervention in case of danger to South Vietnam. Kennedy had sent military advisors, but the US had not initiated any fighting.

The "domino theory" was given as the reason for US intervention. This was the belief that if one Southeast Asian country fell to communism, others would follow like dominoes.

In mid 1963, the US supported a coup, which overthrew neutral South Vietnam leader Diem on November 1, 1963.

By 1964, South Vietnam was again about to fall. An incident on the Gulf of Tonkin provided an excuse for escalating the war. On August 2, 1964, an American destroyer in international waters, which was conducting electronic espionage, was attacked by North Vietnamese torpedo boats. It was unharmed. A second US destroyer joined them, and both ships claimed to have been attacked again on August 4.

Basis of Escalation Was Proven a Lie

This claim of a second attack was later proven to be a lie, but based on this claim, Johnson asked the congress to support the Tonkin Gulf Resolution, a blank check to the executive to conduct retaliatory military operations. There were only two dissenting votes.

Johnson ordered bombing of North Vietnam. After three years, the only apparent result was massive civilian death and destruction of the countryside.

In April 1965, Johnson sent 50,000 ground troops to Vietnam, supposedly to protect air bases there. More ground troops were sent later.

Public Not Told when Defense Tactics Changed to Search and Destroy

The American public was never told when the US strategy changed from static defense to search and destroy.

Total expenses in 1965 alone for the Vietnam war were $100 billion. By 1969, 550,000 troops were sent to Vietnam.

In addition to bombs, the US used chemical warfare including napalm, white phosphorous, and defoliants like Agent Orange.

Draft Falls on Poor

President Johnson drafted American youth. Upper and middle-class youth avoided service in several ways, and America's poor and minority groups ended up bearing the burden of the draft.

Protests at home put the US in a state of near-insurrection. "Teach-ins", protests, and marches on Washington were common.

Johnson Orders Peace Movement Infiltrated by CIA

President Johnson thought the peace movement was infiltrated by communists and ordered the FBI and CIA to conduct an illegal domestic infiltration of the movement.

They returned the information that the peace movement was real and sprang from ordinary citizens.

Despite Johnson's claim that the US was winning, the credibility gap prevented the American public from believing it.

When the Viet Cong mounted the Tet offensive, US confidence was shaken.

Johnson decided to de-escalate and not run for another term.

Lyndon Baines Johnson, president from 1963 to 1969, put through many social programs, but left office unpopular because of the Vietnam War.

Nixon Re-Escalates Vietnam

Richard Nixon promised to end the Vietnam War during his campaign, but he was determined to defeat the communists. After election, he substituted a lottery system for selective service in hopes of defusing opposition.

In the spring of 1970 when the public learned that US troops had massacred more than 300 Vietnamese civilians at My Lai, protests became louder.

Nixon had been wanting to strike Cambodia, and used an April, 1970 coup as an excuse. Ground troops were sent in for three months, but bombing raids lasted until the end of the war.

Six Students Killed by US Troops

Six Kent State and Jackson State University students protesting the war were killed by police and National Guardsmen; 100,000 people marched on Washington D. C.

Nixon Pursues War Despite Congress' Orders

Congress repealed the Gulf of Tonkin resolution which had given Johnson authority to act in Vietnam. Nixon brushed their action aside, saying that as commander in chief he could do anything he deemed necessary to protect the lives of American troops still in Vietnam, and that congress' action was "without binding force or effect."

Deficit financing of the war caused uncontrolled inflation.

The US began to withdraw troops, further demoralizing the men who remained. They knew they were dying for a cause people at home did not support.

In 1972, Nixon ordered massive bombing. Beginning December 12, for 12 days American B-52s bombed Hanoi and Haiphong. Fifteen B-52s were shot down, 44 pilots captured, 1,600 civilians killed, a hospital destroyed, and 36,000 tons of bombs dropped.

Agreement Reached Without South Vietnam

Both sides were then ready to negotiate. An agreement was reached, which South Vietnam leader Thieu refused to sign. Nixon warned that if he resisted, the US would withdraw all aid. Thieu did not sign but neither did he resist.

The agreement provided for US withdrawal and return of its prisoners of war, but left all political negotiations for the North Vietnamese and South Vietnamese governments to settle themselves. The terms left unresolved the supposedly major issue of the war, that is, who would govern South Vietnam.

The US promised to help rebuild North Vietnam.

Both Sides Violate Agreement, Grab More Land

Both sides quickly violated the agreement and tried to seize more land. Nixon continued to bomb Cambodia and was still determined to win.

Watergate Changes Nixon's Plans

Watergate derailed Nixon's plans. Congress passed a bill requiring that hostilities cease by August 15, 1973.

They also passed the War Powers Act over Nixon's veto, which required the president to inform congress within 48 hours of deployment of US military forces overseas, and to withdraw them within 60 days in the absence of congressional endorsement.

South Vietnam Declares Third War, Asks for US Aid Again

South Vietnam's leader Thieu declared the start of a third war in January, thinking that the US would come to his aid. Nixon might have, but the Watergate crisis forced him to resign in August, 1974.

The US cut back their aid from $2.56 billion in 1973 to $907 million in 1974 and $700 million in 1975.

Congress Says No to Ford's Request for Aid

New president Gerald Ford asked for $400 million in aid for South Vietnam, but the congress refused. Thieu resigned and fled the country. His successor surrendered unconditionally on April 30, 1975.

Domino Theory Proves False

The domino theory, which was the justification for the war, proved invalid. No more nations in Southeast Asia embraced communism.

War Kills Millions, Decimates US Economy

Inflation caused by war expenditure decimated the US economy for the next eight years.

Two to three million Indochinese were killed, over 100,000 Americans were killed, the countryside was devastated, more bombs were dropped than in all of World War II, and the war cost the US $150 billion.

No Resolution to Conflict

In 1976, Vietnam was made into one nation and ruled by the northern faction. China attacked Vietnam in 1978, and more than 1.4 million Vietnamese fled by boat; 725,000 settled in the United States.

Hanoi Demands War Reparations

Vietnam invaded Cambodia in 1978. Hanoi continued to demand the war reparations the US had promised North Vietnam.

Pentagon Papers Say War Misrepresented to US Citizens

A secret study was done by the US Department of Defense in 1967-69, known as the Pentagon Papers. The study stated that the US government had misrepresented its role in Southeast Asia to the American people, and it criticized policies that led to the Vietnam War.

Daniel Ellsburg released the study to the New York Times in 1971. They began publishing a series of excerpts. The Department of Justice ordered publication halted on grounds of national security. The supreme court ruled against the Department of Justice and the articles were published in book form.

Whistle Blower Accused of Theft, Espionage, Conspiracy

Ellsburg was indicted for theft, espionage and conspiracy, but charges were dropped in 1973 when it became known that Nixon's administration had burglarized the office of Ellsburg's psychiatrist hoping to find information to use against Ellsburg.

Watergate Ends Nixon's Term

Beginning with Roosevelt, the presidency had become the most powerful agency of government. Both Lyndon Johnson and Richard Nixon seemed willing to put these awesome powers to full use.

Nixon operated on the principle that federal officials could violate the law if he told them to. On June 17, 1972, members of his Special Investigations Unit, which he created without congressional authorization, were arrested while burglarizing the Democratic Party's national offices in the Watergate building in Washington D.C.

The president directed an all-out effort to cover up the ties between the Watergate burglars and his office. The cover-up was an obstruction of justice, a felony.

Previously, Nixon's vice president, Spiro T. Agnew, had resigned because it was discovered he had accepted a bribe. Several others were indicted and/or convicted for burglary, forgery, illegal wiretapping and electronic surveillance, perjury, obstruction of justice, bribery, and other offenses.

Months of televised congressional hearings on the burglaries failed to uncover the fact that Nixon had directed the cover-up. Not until the Supreme Court ordered Nixon to turn over his tapes to congress did the truth come out that he had directly approved it. Nixon resigned before congress could impeach him.

Wage and Price Freeze Hardly Noticed

Nixon's wage and price freeze is hardly remembered in the shadow of Watergate.

"Tricky Dick" Richard Nixon, president from 1969 to 1974, is remembered for his part in Vietnam and for directly approving the Watergate break-in and cover-up.

President Ford Pardons Nixon

Vice president Gerald Ford stepped up to the presidency when Nixon resigned on August 9, 1974. One of his first acts was to grant Nixon a full pardon for any crimes he may have committed while in office.

Ford himself had been appointed vice president in 1973 when Nixon had to replace Agnew, who resigned because of bribery and income tax evasion charges. Nixon used the 25th Amendment as the basis for his appointment.

This was the first time this procedure had been used. Ford was the only president who had not been elected to either the vice presidency or the presidency.

Inflation combined with recession, caused by deficit spending to pay for the Vietnam War cut into the buying power of citizens. Ford did not get along well with the Democratic congress. He vetoed 61 bills during his two and a half years as president. Twelve were overridden.

Ford continued the foreign policy of Nixon. Ford dispatched a small force of Marines to recapture the US freighter Mayaguez and its crew, which had been seized by Cambodian forces.

Ford lost the 1976 election to Jimmy Carter and retired from public office.

Gerald Ford had never had ambitions for a national office. Nixon appointed him as vice president after Spiro T. Agnew was forced to resign. He became president when Nixon resigned to avoid impeachment.

Jimmy Carter Imposes Grain Embargo

Jimmy Carter served as president from 1977 to 1981. He had to deal with soaring inflation, oil and gasoline shortages, Americans taken hostage in Iran, and with the Soviet invasion of Afghanistan a month later.

Carter responded to the Afghanistan invasion with a grain embargo against the Soviets and a US boycott of the

1980 Olympic Games in Moscow. The grain embargo sent grain prices down sharply, and many farmers considered making fuel alcohol from their grain rather than sell it on a depressed market subject to embargo at any time.

Iranian Rescue Mission Fails

A failed mission to rescue the Iranian hostages led to doubts of US military skills, and led to the resignation of Secretary of State Cyrus Vance.

Carter Orders CIA Curtailed

Concern arose about the CIA. Between 1950 and 1973 the CIA had carried out extensive mind-control experiments at universities, prisons, and hospitals. Also, a special commission headed by Nelson Rockefeller found that the CIA had tried to assassinate several foreign leaders, including Fidel Castro, and had tried to prevent Salvadore Allende from winning elections in Chile and later tried to oust him from power.

In 1977, Carter placed tighter restrictions on the CIA. Controls were later placed on wiretapping and opening of mail of US citizens and resident aliens.

Carter, through personal diplomacy, signed the second Strategic Arms Limitation Treaty (Salt II) with the USSR in 1979. The Senate never ratified it.

Carter pushed through the return of the Panama Canal to Panama.

Carter was elected partly because he didn't belong to the establishment in Washington. He owed no favors. As a Washington D. C. cab driver explained to visiting farmers, Carter didn't owe anybody in Washington anything, but Washington didn't owe Carter anything either.

Jimmy Carter, a Georgia peanut farmer, was president from 1977 to 1981. His term was marred by the Iranian hostage crisis, the Russian invasion of Afghanistan, and the grain embargo against the Soviet Union.

Ronald Reagan Declares Economy in Crisis

Ronald Reagan began his presidency in 1981 by declaring that the economy was in a state of crisis requiring bold measures.

He announced that his plan for revitalization would unleash the pent-up energies of entrepreneurs, unleash investment and promote non-inflationary growth.

His plan, or as some say, the plan of his conservative theorists, included sharp budget cuts in social aid, tax cuts, especially for the high income sector, and deregulation of industry. His massive defense spending negated budget cuts elsewhere, however.

In 1982 the US experienced the worst depression since the 1930s. High interest rates, 11% unemployment, and an annual federal deficit of $117 billion (almost twice as high as ever before), and tight money policies from the Federal Reserve prevailed.

Beginning in 1983, the economy rebounded for some, but not for others. Rural America, farmers, and the old industrial regions of the midwest were left in depression.

Number of Poor Increase

In the first part of the 1980s, the number of poor people increased 40% (adding 8.4 million people). One out of every four Americans lived below the poverty level.

Defense spending and tax cuts for corporations and the wealthy kept the economy booming for some. At the end of his term, Republicans boasted that he had helped create 16.5 million jobs, cut unemployment to a 17-year low, brought double-digit inflation down to 4%, and raised the gross national product by a third.

Debt and Trade Deficit at All Time High

Democrats, on the other hand, accused Reagan of promoting prosperity for the rich at the expense of the poor and of mortgaging the nation's future. They pointed out that the number of poor people below the poverty level rose by more than 8 million, combined with cuts of $50 billion in social welfare programs, reduced subsidized housing to a level that made "homelessness" part of the nation's vocabulary, and that the number of Americans with no health insurance rose to 37 million. The cost of servicing the national debt rose from 8.9% of federal outlays to 14.8%, and the US had become a debtor nation for the first time since 1914.

Wealth Didn't Trickle Down

The wealth did not trickle down as promised. Many at the bottom never even got a shower.

Reagan Gives Covert Aid to Contras

Reagan sent military advisors and money to El Salvador to stop a communist revolt. He gave covert aid to anti-government rebels (Contras) despite a congressional ban on this aid.

Reagan Sends Troops to Lebanon

Reagan sent troops to Lebanon to keep the peace in 1982 but withdrew them after 241 marines were killed in a surprise bomb attack in October, 1983.

Reagan Invades Grenada

Reagan ordered invasion of the island of Grenada in October, 1983, and overthrew the country's anti-American dictator, supposedly to head off a Cuban and Soviet military buildup. Eleven days earlier the Grenadan prime minister had been murdered by the Marxist New Jewel Movement. Troops left two months later after an interim government was established. Oliver North, later of Iran Contra fame, played a key role in planning the Grenada invasion. General Norman Schwarzkopf, later of Desert Storm fame, led the attack.

CIA Tries to Overthrow Sandanistas

US troops were sent to Central America. The CIA worked openly to overturn the Sandanista regime in Nicaragua. The US deployed a new batch of nuclear missiles to Europe, raising Soviet distrust to such a pitch that they froze arms control talks.

US Bombs Libya

The US bombed targets in Tripoli and Benghazi in 1986 in retaliation for allegedly directing terrorist attacks.

US warplanes shot down two Libyan MIG-23s over the Mediterranean. Only days before, the US had claimed Libya was about to complete a factory to make chemical weapons.

Administration Caught Selling Arms to Iran, Giving Money to Contras

Reagan was embarrassed when administration officials were caught selling arms to Iran and giving part of the money to anti-Sandanista rebels (Contras) in Nicaragua. Congressional investigation led to prosecution of National Security Advisor John M. Poindexter and Marine Lt. Col. Oliver North.

Reagan Claims No Knowledge of Contra Affair

Reagan claimed he did not know of the Iran-Contra Affair. Critics were left wondering if he was lying or was a poor manager. Reagan refused to turn over his diaries, citing executive privilege. A US district court upheld Reagan's refusal.

North told congress in 1987 that the operation was authorized by his superiors, and that he assumed President Reagan knew the plan, but had never discussed it with him personally. He said CIA director William Casey had approved the action enthusiastically.

North was indicted in 1988 for conspiracy to defraud the government. Vice Admiral John M. Poindexter, retired Air Force Major General Richard Secord, and an Iranian-American businessman were also charged.

North Convicted

After two years of congressional testimony, pretrial argument, and finally a trial, North was convicted of obstructing congress, destroying documents, and accepting an illegal gratuity (a security system for his home.) North was fined $150,000 and ordered to perform 1200 hours of community service, was given a three year suspended sentence and placed on probation.

North Testifies Against Poindexter; North's Conviction Overturned

All three convictions were suspended after North appeared as a prosecution witness against his former boss, John M. Poindexter. Independent counsel Lawrence Walsh tried to get a federal appeals court to reconsider, but in May, 1991, the US Supreme Court upheld the decision. Walsh was forced to abandon five years of prosecution effort.

During Poindexter's trial, Reagan was called to testify in a videotaped closed courtroom. He said he had not ordered any illegal activities. Frequent memory lapses punctuated his testimony.

On the economic side, the stock market collapsed in October, 1987.

President Ronald Reagan, president from 1981 to 1989, is remembered for the Iran Contra Affair, which he claims he knew nothing about, the invasion of Grenada, and a huge increase in debt and trade deficit.

George Bush Invades Panama, Kuwait

George Bush ordered the invasion of Panama in 1989 to overthrow its president, Manuel Noriega, supported in previous times by Bush.

In 1991 he sent 700,000 American troops to the Persian Gulf to defend Kuwait from Iraqi occupation. When Iraq, formerly supported by Bush, refused to withdraw, he ordered a massive bombing attack and ground assault; 1800 aircraft and 100 ships were used.

Bush found it difficult to give one single overriding reason for attacking Iraq. Critics asked if the war was to secure oil supplies or to oppose aggression by Iraq. Other countries more directly affected refused to commit forces.

When King Fahd of Saudi Arabia first invited American troops onto Saudi ground, they were deployed with light, defensive weaponry, and the operation was called Desert Shield. They were soon enforced with heavy weapons and more infantry. In November, 1990, Bush announced a force buildup for offensive action, and changed the name to Desert Storm.

Bush Says He Doesn't Need Congress' Approval

President Bush told congress he would like to have their approval, but it was not at all necessary. Congress voted to authorize "all necessary means" by a narrow margin.

Iraqi Leader Left Intact

Saddam Hussein, Iraqi leader, was said to have believed from the beginning that the US was committed to going to war, regardless of his actions.

Bush terminated the war without toppling Saddam Hussein. He was left in place as Iraqi leader. Iraq was allowed to rescue military equipment and personnel that were later used against Shiite and Kurdish citizens.

The Defense intelligence agency estimated that 100,000 Iraqi soldiers died, 300,000 were wounded, and 60,000 taken prisoner. Kuwait was decimated, littered with thousands of land mines and polluted with 730 burning oil wells and giant pools of spilled oil.

The US sent the US Corps of Engineers to help reconstruct Kuwait.

In 1994 the public learned that 20,000 of the 700,000 servicemen sent to the Persian Gulf by President Bush were ill with the so-called "Gulf War Syndrome," and that as high as 77% had transmitted the disease to their spouses. 65% of their postwar babies had medical problems, including deformities. Many of the vets were confined to wheelchairs as the disease progressed. The Veterans Administration denied disability payments because the disease manifested itself more than a year after the war. Researchers feared the contagious illness had entered the nation's blood supply and was comparable to the AIDS epidemic.

30,000 Troops Sent to Somalia

Bush sent 30,000 troops to Somalia in 1992 to ensure delivery of food aid.

Bush's administration was plagued by economic recession despite the war on Iraq.

President George Bush sent 500,000 troops to war with Iraq, a country he had once supported, but was hard put to come up with an overriding reason for doing so. Bush was former head of the CIA.

Bill Clinton Elected

Former Arkansas governor Bill Clinton campaigned with lawyer wife Hillary and running mate environmentalist Al Gore saying it was time for a new generation of leadership. He offered plans for economic growth, health-care reform, defense conversion, education renewal and welfare reform.

Shortly after taking office, Clinton asked congress for $246 billion in new taxes, $169 billion to stimulate the economy, and a general spending cut of $257 billion, including defense cuts.

Air drops of food and other needs were made in Bosnia, in the throes of war. He urged greater aid to Russia and former Soviet Union countries. He was the catalyst in getting peace agreements between Israel and the PLO.

He sent several thousand troops to Haiti to re-install ousted president Aristide. A few weeks later Saddam Hussein of Iraq started moving troops toward the Kuwait border, and Clinton sent about 50,000 troops to the Persian Gulf to force Hussein to withdraw.

In an address to the nation, he said he had the right to send troops and cited previous presidents' actions. Clinton taught constitutional law before becoming president.

Bill Clinton, elected president in 1992, wanted to provide a new generation of leadership. In 1993, his first year in office, the poverty rate had climbed to 15.1%, and the gap between rich and poor widened. 40% of all poor people were children. Poverty rate was highest in the South, in rural areas, and among Blacks.

Chapter Thirteen

War Money and Peace Money

When the American People finally understand the difference between wealth and money on the one hand and debt and credit on the other, there will be an immediate revolution against the government. - Eugene Schroder

We must understand one critical concept before we can comprehend the nature of money and credit: there are two kinds of money that can exist in this country, "war money" and "peace money."

War Money Represents Debt;
Peace Money Represents Prosperity

War money always represents debt and is usually applied against the losers or enemies as a reparation of war. Authority to compel performance on this debt is always enforced through the military or police power.

Peace money represents wealth, prosperity and freedom, but never debt.

Peace Money Has Seen Limited Use

First we will look at peace money, as it has had limited use in this country and certainly has not been seen since March 9, 1933. The Constitution states: "Congress shall have the power to coin the money and regulate the value thereof" and "to fix the standard of weights and measures." It goes on to say that "No state shall ... make anything but gold and silver coin a tender in payment of debt."

The fact that those metals are rare, durable, and cannot be counterfeited is important. More important, however, is the fact that new money could be created and brought into circulation without creating debt and interest on that debt. Anyone, through hard work and a pick and shovel, could go into the countryside and mine the heavy metals. Then they could take the metals to the mint where they were standardized, then stamped into official United States of America money. Mother nature and hard work provided for the new wealth. Money was made and created. The people as a whole could circulate that money free from debt to anyone. New money was continually being created to provide for growth in the economy as the population grew.

In theory this money and mechanism of creation works well. There are some problems, however. For example, if the economy needs and wants to grow and there is not an adequate supply of new metals being discovered, a shortage of money results which slows growth. Other problems can also obviously arise. These problems pale into utter insignificance when compared to the destructive nature of war money.

War Changes Entire Structure of Country

When the dogs of war are loosed, a country undergoes a major revision. Caution is thrown to the wind. The government immediately assumes control over all industry and agriculture. The young men of the nation are conscripted into fighting units.

Labor is regulated and pricing is controlled. Communication and transportation are controlled and regulated. The entire economic and social structure of the country goes under government control. The constitution and peacetime laws are suspended.

Paper War Money Finances Destruction

There is an urgent need for guns, bombs, tanks, ships, planes, missiles, trucks and food. The entire economy is placed into overdrive to produce this material that will be thrown into war and immediately destroyed. Obviously this operation requires money, a lot of money. Thus we see the origin of "war powers" and "war money."

War money always takes the form of paper currency and always represents a debt or obligation upon the people. Normally, the prize taken from enemies is used to help give value to this currency. When the war is over the victor claims the captured nation and people as prize and these people are required to pay for the damages and cost of the war. The enemy is held in bondage or debt until the war costs are paid and the war currency is retired.

Colonies Won Independence but Got Stuck with the Bill

The first currency issued by the colonies after they declared independence from England was the Continental Dollar. It was a war currency issued to fight the revolutionary war. The Continental Congress, needing to finance an army but lacking taxing power, turned to the printing press. These dollars were government bonds that promised to pay at a later date. However, at the end of the war the colonies failed to sufficiently defeat England to a degree that they could claim it as prize.

We succeeded in gaining our independence but we had no one to pay the costs. Ultimately the war currency became worthless, giving rise to the saying "Not worth a Continental." Inside speculators purchased this money for a few cents on the dollar. A short time later congress proposed a plan to reissue the bonds and pay them off at face value.

The government implemented tonnage and duties on ships and imports to raise revenue. They also imposed an excise tax on the sale of liquor. Farmers of the west violently disagreed with the federal power of taxation over them for this purpose, giving rise to Shays Rebellion. The first rebellion in the United States was a result of war money and the federal power to tax as a means to retire that money.

The situation worsened when John Jay, Secretary of State under John Adams, signed a secret treaty with Great Britain agreeing to pay the British war reparations. When the treaty was made known, there was widespread political unrest. The French, who had financed the colonies in the war against Britain, were also violently irritated by this treaty. France and England drifted towards war.

The Federalist party under Adams and Jay, who had remained united with Great Britain, retaliated against the anti-Federalist French sympathizers by pushing through the Alien and Sedition Acts in 1798. One section of this act as it was originally written was said to have declared that "every Frenchman was an enemy to the United States and that to give him aid or comfort was treason," punishable with death. Another section declared that "any person who defamed the government of the United States should suffer punishment by imprisonment or fine." It was feared that this would cause a civil war between the northern British sympathizers and the southern French sympathizers.

Virginia and Kentucky passed resolutions saying their general assemblies were fully resolved to maintain and defend the constitution of the United States and the constitutions of the states against every aggressor, either foreign or domestic. The states, it said, had the right to interpose in case of deliberate, palpable, and dangerous exercise of powers not granted to the federal government by the constitution. Civil war was averted when out of this turmoil Thomas Jefferson was elected president. (For a full accounting of the devastating effect of this war currency, one should read *Constitutional Development* by Carl Brent Swisher, Riverside Press, Cambridge, Mass.)

The American people won independence in the revolutionary war against Great Britain but almost lost it again through the war money.

War Money Financed Civil War

The next "war money" was issued by Abraham Lincoln and Jefferson Davis during the civil war. Lincoln issued the "Greenbacks" to finance the north while Davis issued the "Confederate money" to finance the south. The division between the north and south was finally complete. When the south seceded from the union, they formed a new nation, a new government, raised their own army and issued their own war money.

Losing South Became Prize of War

The south was defeated and became a prize of war. The 1867 act entitled "An Act to Provide for the More Efficient Government of the States in Rebellion" made the southern states a captured nation (prize of war) until they ratified the 14th Amendment.

Section I of this law made the states permanently subject to the military authority of the federal government. It also applied the reparation of war to pay the cost of the war and retire the war money. The southern states were divided into five military districts.

Section 4 of this law said that the validity of the public debt of the United States, including debts incurred for payments of pensions and bounties for services in suppressing insurrection or rebellion, shall not be questioned. It also provided that neither the United States nor any state would assume or pay any debt or obligation incurred in aid of insurrection or rebellion against the United States, or any claim for the loss or emancipation of any slave, and that all such debts, obligations and claims should be held illegal and void.

South Required to Pay Costs of War

The south, the enemy of the United States, was required to pay all costs and the confederate money was declared void.

The 14th Amendment was ratified by military districts and was strictly a war measure. Under the captured property acts, revenue agents (better known as carpetbaggers) were unleashed on the south. In all reality the southern nation has yet to recover from this devastation. The losers pay the cost of war.

Federal Reserve Formed to Finance World War I

Congress enacted the Federal Reserve Act on December 23, 1913. Great Britain had formally declared war status against Germany. The United States, formally allied with Great Britain, went on unofficial war footing. The Federal Reserve was created to issue war money to finance World War I.

Income Tax Passed to Cover War Money

The 16th Amendment establishing an income tax was passed to provide taxing power to cover this war money. The government, as is always the case, assumed control over the economic and social affairs of the country.

Trading With Enemy Act Controls Finances of Enemy

The United States formally entered the war in 1917, and it is here that our current dilemma with war money began. Congress immediately passed "An Act to Define, Regulate, and Punish Trading With The Enemy." (October 6, 1917). This act, patterned after the alien and sedition act, identified any German living within the borders of the US or any ally of Germany as an enemy of the US. The act gave the president total authoritarian power over these enemies. Section B of the act gave the president power to control all financial transactions of enemies. Specifically exempted from this act were all US citizens and their transactions.

At this point the US government was not only issuing war money (Federal Reserve notes) but also totally controlling enemy transactions, as well as controlling domestic agriculture, industry and labor. A full accounting of this period is given in *War Powers of the Executive in the United States* by Clarence A. Bordahl, 1920, University of Illinois.

Federal Reserve Notes Manipulated; Boom and Bust Results

Federal Reserve notes were not retired at the termination of the war. In 1921 these notes were severely restricted in the southern and western states, resulting in widespread bankruptcy, business failure and despair. This caused peacetime money (gold and silver) to be removed from the southern and western states, as well as other states. (Refer to the Congressional Record of August 15, 1921).

The war money was then greatly expanded once more, and the economy experienced tremendous growth. The period of excessive speculation and easy money is known as the roaring twenties. The speculative bubble collapsed in 1929, again resulting in widespread bankruptcy and business failures. This condition led directly into the Great Depression.

Government Gains Financial Control Over People

President Franklin Roosevelt was inaugurated on March 4, 1933. In his inaugural address he signaled his intention to assume war powers to deal with the depression. On March 6 he issued Proclamation 2039, which had been proposed on March 3 by the Federal Reserve Bank of New York. He based his authority on the Trading With the Enemy Act, an act of war. Approval of this act on March 9 meant that the people of the United States were now to be treated the same as enemies.

With this act, the president gained power to issue emergency war money in the form of Federal Reserve Bank Notes.

This act was an exercise of war upon the American people.

Government Seized Peacetime Money; Exempted Banks from Law

Why was this done? Because the people were lined up outside the banks demanding their gold and silver coins that they had deposited in the banks. The banks could not pay the depositors back the gold and silver coin. Roosevelt, in failing to apply the laws of the United States against the banks and bankers, in effect gave them titles of nobility by holding them up as exempt from the law. He, in effect, exempted the banks from the laws and declared the American people as the enemy. The American people were stripped of any remedy against the banks and bankers.

The banks were closed and all peacetime money (gold and silver) was seized. The government and the banks remain, to this day, the true debtors. The peacetime money was never returned to the American people.

New Money Based on Total Debt

Title IV of the Emergency Act of March 9, 1933, provided that upon deposits with the US Treasury either (a) direct obligations of the US (being taxpayer obligations or national debt) or (b) notes, drafts, bills of exchange and bank acceptances (being private debt), the banks would be issued circulating notes in blank (emergency war script).

The Congressional Record of March 9, 1933 contains discussion of this.

> *Congressman McFadden*. I would like to ask the chairman of the committee if this is a plan to change the holding of the security back of the Federal Reserve notes to the Treasury of the United States rather than the Federal Reserve agent.
>
> *Chairman Steagall.* The provision is for the issuance of Federal Reserve bank notes; and not the Federal Reserve notes; and the security back is the obligations, notes, drafts, bills of exchange, bank acceptances, outlined in the section to which the gentleman has referred.
>
> *Congressman McFadden*. Then the new circulation is to be Federal Reserve bank notes and not Federal Reserve notes. Is that true?
>
> *Chairman Steagall.* Insofar as the provisions of this section are concerned. Yes.
>
> *Congressman Britten.* From my observations of the bill as it was read to the house, it would appear that the amount of bank notes that might be issued by the Federal Reserve System is not limited. That will depend entirely upon the amount of collateral that is presented from time to time for exchange of bank notes. Is that not correct?
>
> *Congressman Patman*. The money will be worth 100 cents on the dollar because it is backed by the credit of the nation. It will represent a mortgage on all the homes and other property of all the people in the nation.

We became chattel property, the prize of war, with this act. The people and all their property became the security that back the government's Federal Reserve bank notes.

By Definition, Debt Can Never Be Repaid

The next section of Title IV section 401 of this act of March 9, 1933 provides that the estimated value of the people's debt can be discounted 10%:

> When such circulating notes are issued against the security of the obligations of the United States the amount of such circulating notes shall be equal to the face value of the direct obligations of the United States so deposited as security; and, when issued against the security of notes, drafts, bills of exchange, bankers acceptances acquired under the provision of this Act, the amount thereof shall be equal to not more than 90 percent of the estimated value of such notes, drafts, bills of exchange, and bankers acceptances so deposited as security.

We can write algebraic equations that show the relationship between the total debt and the total currency issued.

A (National Debt) + B (Private Debt) = D (Total Debt)

But the amount of currency issued is

A + (B - 10B%) = C (Total Currency Printed)

Therefore:

D(Debt) = C(Total Currency) + 10% B(Private Debt)
or
C (Total Currency) = D(Debt) - 10%B(Private Debt)

These equations show that the amount of currency issued is never as great as the total debt. The debt can never be repaid, because there will never be enough currency issued to repay it. The American people and their property are in a state of permanent bondage.

Debt Grows Exponentially

From 1933 we can watch the growth of the aggregate debt (both public and private debt). Because the discount can not be repaid, it must be "rolled over" and added to more principal either in the form of A or B. The discount and the interest charged begins to grow at an exponential rate.

The total debt in 1990 was $26 trillion, as reported by the Federal Reserve of Chicago in "Two Faces of Debt." We have only about $500 billion in circulating currency with which to pay that debt.

Are the American people in a state of bondage? Remember the enemy losers pay the cost of war. We lost that war over 61 years ago and never fired a shot.

Who Owes the Debt?

The US Senate in 1973 made the following statement: "Since March 9, 1933 the United States has been in a state of declared national emergency." (Senate Report 93-549 -1973).

The emergency measures embodied in the Emergency Banking Relief Act, Proclamation #2039, and the state of emergency confirmed by the congress on March 9, 1933, have now been codified into law in Title 12 U.S. Code Section 95(b).

If we cherish our liberty and our freedom, we must terminate this emergency and restore our legitimate debt-and-interest-free peacetime money.

There is no legitimate debt owed by the American people. The government and the Federal Reserve system acting as its agent are the true and lawful debtors to the American people.

War Money

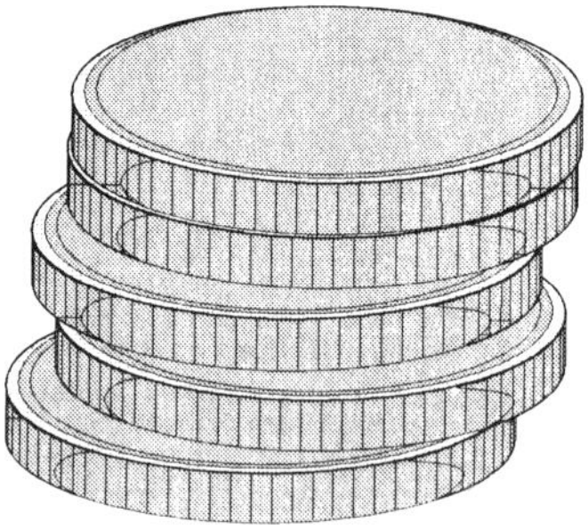

Peacetime Money

Forgotten Constitution

Chapter Fourteen

Healing the Nation

Power over currency continues to be a political tool. The existence of Federal Reserve bank notes backed by the debt of the people is a direct result of war powers.

The Federal Reserve Board, still a quasi-governmental agency, is practically immune from controls, yet its actions determine whether we can send our children to college, buy a new refrigerator, or get a business loan. There is no one watching the fox that guards the hen house.

Each time the country is declared in "emergency", more control is exercised over the everyday lives of Americans. The liberties taken away have never been fully restored at the end of the emergency, and for the last 61 years, the emergency has never ended.

There is little incentive for that "emergency" to be declared at an end because the government would lose its power over the American people.

In management schools, it is recognized that certain types of managers gain a reputation for their heroic actions in time of crisis. These managers are glorified for pulling the fat out of the fire, so to speak.

On the other hand, the manager who plans methodically and organizes well forestalls emergencies before they happen. He never gets glorified as a hero because he never lets the fire get started in the first place.

If the incentive for emergency were taken away from the president and his agencies, we might find more responsibility toward money, foreign policy, and constitutional rights.

It is time to ask for healing of this nation before we go past the point of no return. The government took control of our assets, then our money, and have made deep inroads into controlling our minds. The only thing we have left is our intelligence, reason, and determination. We must hold on to our ability to think freely and clearly.

It is time to take the moral high road - for ourselves, for our children, our grandchildren, and the world.

It is time for each of us to take individual responsibility for our own welfare and our own morality. It is time for us to shoulder the duty and privilege of steering our government on a straight, just and moral path.

It is time for our congress to once again take up the duties they have abdicated. It is time for congress to do their job. It is time for individual members to realize they have the same charges as citizens to lead just and moral lives, and in addition they have duties as leaders to set a good example.

It is time for our judicial system to re-examine the constitutionality of entrenched war and emergency powers, to once again assume their rightful place as one leg of the triangle of shared and balanced powers.

It is time for the president to give up all war and emergency powers and return the United States to constitutional rule.

It is time for all politicians and government employees to realize that the sole purpose of their job is to serve the citizens.

It is time for each of us to regain our self-respect and confidence by realizing that many times the best solutions to our problems are our own resources and ingenuity and hard work, not an appeal to the government. It is time for each of us to challenge injustice in the best way that we can, from wherever we are, using whatever resources we have, every time we can.

No one wants to fight a revolutionary war against the US government. Yet increasingly, US citizens are unwilling to be the pawns of arbitrary and capricious decrees. We have both the right and duty to reclaim our country.

Appendix A

What Can I Do?

If you are satisfied with the way things are, then there is no reason to do anything.

If you are concerned with America's problems, but you have become cynical and think that nothing can be done, then we certainly can empathize. We've all been there at one time or another.

If you think it is unpatriotic to criticize your country, then consider that a loving and dutiful parent corrects his children so they will grow up to be strong and successful.

This country is our baby. Maybe we personally didn't get things in the mess they're in today, but it's our responsibility to correct it. There isn't anyone else to do it. We don't give our children away, and we can't give our country away.

We have levied strong criticisms against the federal government, the unconstitutional use of power, and the system in general. But America is still probably the strongest country in the world. Other peoples envy and emulate us.

What we seek is a way to avoid slipping into the cesspool of stagnation, corruption, and dictatorship that seems to set in with age. We can compare a country with a colony of bacteria. When the population is sparse and nutrients are plentiful, the bacteria grow and multiply rapidly. As the population increases, it uses up all the nutrients and poisons itself with its own waste. The colony of bacteria dies unless it is inoculated into fresh growth medium.

We cannot allow ourselves to be hogtied with red tape, suffocated with bureaucracy, and force-fed poisonous propaganda. The challenge is to keep the country growing and healthy with fresh ideas, ingenuity and action.

We believe that we must take our country back peacefully while we still can.

Although millions have given up because the task seems too great, there are still independent thinkers and activists in America, and millions more waiting for a spark to be ignited.

We can still make up our own minds. We can still read the Constitution. We can still use public and university libraries for research. We can still write to elected office-holders. We can still get involved in political parties, attend meetings, and connect through talk shows and computers online.

Politicians listen to money and votes. That leaves most of us with our votes. However, we can influence others' votes.

Elected officials cannot ignore a groundswell.

A determined and focused resolve finds opportunities for action. To paraphrase a Methodist challenge, do all the good you can everywhere you can every chance you get.

Letters to elected officials make your views known. Address letters to the president, senators and house members as follows:

President ____________
The White House
Washington, D.C. 20500

Senator ______________
U. S. Senate
Washington D. C. 20510

Representative __________
House of Representatives
Washington D.C. 20515

You can get your state officials' names and addresses from either party's political headquarters or from any activist group.

Avoid the appearance of mass-produced letters. If typed or printed, a nice touch is to add a hand-written note in blue ink.

Stick to one subject per letter. Keep it to one page. Make your point but don't muddle the issue. It's good to start with a compliment if you can think of one.

Activist groups have spurred several states to begin to assert their states rights and challenge federal mandates. California has sued the federal government for money to pay for federally mandated programs concerning illegal immigrants. A "Take Texas Back" movement is flourishing in the Lone Star state.

The American Agriculture Movement office in Campo, Colorado has agreed to be a clearinghouse for information on efforts to restore the constitution.

Write or call:

AAM
Box 130
Campo, CO 81029

Phone 719-787-9958

Colorado passed both a Resolution and a Federal Mandate Act challenging federal authority. Passed by the Colorado House and Senate and signed by the Governor in 1994, both could become model legislation for other states to enact.

If many states pass such laws and resolutions, the federal government will be strongly challenged to stop issuing decrees outside its constitutional jurisdiction.

Colorado's Federal Mandate Act

Colorado's Federal Mandate Act (Article 78) amends Colorado state code.

It reads in part:

24-78-102. Legislative declaration. (1) (a) In enacting this Article, the General Assembly employs its legislative authority to establish that the people of the State of Colorado, acting through their elected officials in Colorado State Government, have the responsibility and authority to establish policy in and for Colorado pertaining to Federal programs mandated in Federal Statutes.

(b) The intent of the General Assembly is to assure the primacy of the State of Colorado's legal and political authority to implement in and for Colorado the policy mandated by Federal Statutes and to vigorously challenge and scrutinize the extent and scope of authority asserted by Federal Executive Branch agencies when Federal Agency actions and interpretations are inconsistent with Colorado policy and exceed the lawful authority of the Federal Government or are not required by Federal Law.

(c) In this connection the Colorado General Assembly finds and declares that:

(I) The power to implement Federal policies in and for Colorado is central to the ability of the people of Colorado to govern themselves under a Federal system of government; and

(II) Any implementation of Federal Policies in and for Colorado by Federal Executive Branch agencies that is contrary to fundamental notions of federalism and self-determination must be identified and countered.

(2) The General Assembly further finds and declares that:

(a) There is an urgent need to modify Federal Mandates because the implementation of these mandates by the state wastes the financial resources of local governments, the citizens of Colorado, and the state and does not properly respect the rights of the state, local governments, and citizens.

(b) The State Government has an obligation to the public to do what is necessary to protect the rights of Colorado citizens under Federal Law while minimizing or eliminating any additional cost or regulatory burden on any citizen of the state.

(c) The Tenth Amendment of the United States Constitution directs that powers that are not delegated to the United States are reserved to the states or to the people. Colorado, as one of the sovereign states within the union, has constitutional authority to enact laws protecting the environment of the state and safeguarding the public health, safety, and welfare of the citizens of Colorado. However, this authority has too often been ignored by the Federal Government, as the Federal Government has intruded more and more into areas that must be left to the states. It is essential that the dilution of the authority of state and local governments be halted and that the provisions of the Tenth Amendment be accorded proper respect.

(d) Current Federal Regulatory Mandates, as reflected in Federal Administrative Regulations, guidelines, and policies, often do not reflect the realities of the Rocky Mountain Region, and Federal Regulators frequently do not understand the needs and priorities of the citizens of Colorado.

(c) The citizens of the state can create and wish to create innovative solutions to Colorado's problems, but the current manner in which legal challenges to state policies and Federal programmatic substitutions of state programs are handled does not allow the state the flexibility it needs. It is not possible for the State of Colorado to effectively and efficiently implement the provisions of Federal Statutes unless the burden to prove the insufficiency of the State's efforts to implement Federal requirements is shifted to the person or agency who asserts such insufficiency.

(f) The provisions of this article will better balance the exercise of the powers of the Federal Government and the powers reserved to the States. In addition, the application of this article ultimately will bring about greater protection for the State and the Nation, because it will direct the state to implement Federal Statutes at the least possible cost, thereby freeing more moneys for other needs.

(g) The purpose of this part I is to ensure that Federal Mandates implemented in Colorado comply with State Policy as established by the General Assembly.

24-78-103. Definitions. As used in this part I, unless the context otherwise requires:

(1) "Executive Committee" means the Executive Committee of the legislative council established pursuant to Section 2-3-301 (1), C. R. S.

(2) "Federal Statute" means a Federal Statute that is in accord with the United States Constitution imposing mandates on state or local governments, which may include, but is not limited to, the following:

(a) The Federal "Safe Drinking Water Act", 42 U.S.C. Sec. 300f, et seq. as amended;

(b) The Federal "Clean Air Act", 42 U.S.C. Sec. 7401, et. seq., as amended;

(c) The "Federal Water Pollution Control Act", 33 U.S.C. Sec. 1251, et. seq., as amended:

(d) The Federal "Solid Waste Disposal Act", 42 U. S. C. Sec. 3251, et seq., as amended;

(e) The Federal "Resource Conservation and Recovery Act of 1976", 42 U.S.C. Sec. 6901, et. seq., as amended;

(f) The Federal "Comprehensive Environmental Response, Compensation, and Liability Act of 1980", 42 U.S.C. Sec. 9601, et. seq., as amended;

(g) The Federal "Superfund Amendments and Reauthorization Act of 1986", P. L. 99-499, as amended;

(h) The Federal "Endangered Species Act of 1973", 16 U.S.C. Sec. 1531, et. seq., as amended.

(i) The Federal Asbestos School Hazard Abatement Statute, 20 U.S.C. Sec. 4011, et. seq., as amended;

(j) The Federal "Brady Handgun Violence Prevention Act of 1993", P. L. 101-336, as amended;

(k) The Federal "Commercial Motor Vehicle Safety Act of 1986", 49 U.S.C. Sec. 2501, as amended;

(l) The Federal "Family and Medical Leave Act of 1993", P. L. 103-3, as amended;

(m) The Federal "Emergency Planning and Community Right-To-Know Act", P. L. 99-145 and 99-499, as amended;

(n) The Federal, State and Local Partnership for Education Improvement Program, 20 U.S.C. Sec. 1751, et seq., as amended;

(o) The Federal "National Voter Registration Act of 1993", P. L. 103-31, as amended;

(p) The Federal School Lunch Program and School Breakfast Program, 42 U.S.C. Secs. 1751 and 1773, as amended;

(q) The Federal Social Services and Medicaid Requirements, 42 U.S.C. Sec. 1396 as amended;

(r) Federal Highway Safety Programs;

(s) The Federal "Intermodal Surface Transportation Efficiency Act of 1991":, P. L. 102-240, as amended.

The Act goes on to direct that any state agency making a budget request for a federally mandated state program include in its request citations to the federal or state constitutional provisions that authorize the state program. The General Assembly will determine if federal constitutional authority and state constitutional or statutory authority exist.

Requests for information regarding federal mandates were sent to those with expertise on federal mandates, including college and university faculty, attorneys, and organizations and foundations with an interest in the issues of federalism. The goal was to identify the following: federally mandated actions that could best be done on a state by state basis or that could be resisted because of unique circumstances or unnecessary burdens; legal theories supporting the right of each state to implement or oppose federal mandates based on the state's own policies; and practical methods for the state to fully exercise its own authority in implementing federal mandates.

The last paragraph of the Act states:

> Section 6. Safety clause. The general assembly hereby finds, determines, and declares that this act is necessary for the immediate preservation of the public peace, health, and safety.

Colorado House Joint Resolution 94-1035

The Colorado House and Senate also passed the following joint resolution:

> WHEREAS, The 10th Amendment to the Constitution of the United States reads as follows:
>
> "The powers not delegated to the United States by the Constitution, nor prohibited by it to the States, are reserved to the States respectively, or to the people"; and
>
> WHEREAS, The 10th Amendment defines the total scope of federal power as being that specifically granted by the United States Constitution and no more; and
>
> WHEREAS, The scope of power defined by the 10th Amendment means that the federal government was created by the states specifically to be an agent of the states; and
>
> WHEREAS, Today, in 1994, the states are in fact treated as agents of the federal government, and

WHEREAS, Numerous resolutions have been forwarded to the federal government by the Colorado General Assembly without any response or result from Congress or the federal government; and

WHEREAS, Many federal mandates are directly in violation of the 10th Amendment to the Constitution of the United States; and

WHEREAS, The United States Supreme Court has ruled in New York v. United States, 112 S. Ct. 2408 (1992), that Congress may not simply commandeer the legislative and regulatory processes of the states; and

WHEREAS, A number of proposals now from the previous administrations and some now pending from the present administration and from Congress may further violate the United States Constitution; now, therefore,

Be It Resolved by the House of Representatives of the Fifty-ninth General Assembly of the State of Colorado, the Senate concurring herein:

(1) That the State of Colorado hereby claims sovereignty under the 10th Amendment to the Constitution of the United States over all powers not otherwise enumerated and granted to the federal government by the United States Constitution.

(2) That this serve as a Notice and Demand to the federal government, as our agent, to cease and desist, effective immediately, mandates that are beyond the scope of its constitutionally delegated powers,

Be It Further Resolved, That copies of this Resolution be sent to the President of the United States, the Speaker of the United States House of Representatives, the President of the United States Senate, the Speaker of the House and the President of the Senate of each state's legislature of the United States of America, and Colorado's Congressional delegation.

Who is the better parent? Is it the parent who turns his head while his child misbehaves, or is it the parent who takes that child firmly in hand? Which child will grow up to be disciplined and responsible?

Is America worth our effort?

Appendix B

In Congress, July 4, 1776,

THE UNANIMOUS DECLARATION OF THE THIRTEEN UNITED STATES OF AMERICA

When in the Course of human events, it becomes necessary for one people to dissolve the political bands which have connected them with another, and to assume among the Powers of the earth, the separate and equal station to which the Laws of Nature and of Nature's God entitle them, a decent respect to the opinions of mankind requires that they should declare the causes which impel them to the separation.

We hold these truths to be self-evident, that all men are created equal, that they are endowed by their Creator with certain unalienable Rights, that among these are Life, Liberty, and the pursuit of Happiness.

That to secure these rights, Governments are instituted among Men, deriving their just powers from the consent of the governed.

That whenever any Form of Government becomes destructive of these ends, it is the Right of the People to alter or to abolish it, and to institute new Government, laying its foundation on such principles and organizing its powers in such form, as to them shall seem most likely to effect their Safety and Happiness. Prudence, indeed, will dictate that Governments long established should not be changed for light and transient causes; and accordingly all experience hath shown, that mankind are more disposed to suffer, while evils are sufferable, than to right themselves by abolishing the forms to which they are accustomed. But when a long train of abuses and usurpations, pursuing invariably the same Object, evinces a design to reduce them under absolute Despotism, it is their right, it is their duty, to throw off such Government, and to provide new Guards for their future security.

Such has been the patient sufferance of these Colonies; and such is now the necessity which constrains them to alter their former Systems of Government. The history of the present King of Great Britain is a history of repeated injuries and usurpations, all having in direct object the establishment of an absolute Tyranny over these States. To prove this, let Facts be submitted to a candid world.

He has refused his Assent to Laws, the most wholesome and necessary for the public good.

He has forbidden his Governors to pass Laws of immediate and pressing importance, unless suspended in their operation till his Assent should be obtained; and when so suspended, he has utterly neglected to attend to them.

He has refused to pass other Laws for the accommodation of large districts of people, unless those people would relinquish the right of Representation in the Legislature, a right inestimable to them and formidable to tyrants only.

He has called together legislative bodies at places unusual, uncomfortable, and distant from the depository of their public Records, for the sole purpose of fatiguing them into compliance with his measures.

He has dissolved Representative Houses repeatedly, for opposing with manly firmness his invasions on the rights of the people.

He has refused for a long time, after such dissolutions, to cause others to be elected; whereby the Legislative powers, incapable of Annihilation, have returned to the People at large for their exercise; the State remaining in the mean time exposed to all the dangers of invasion from without, and convulsions within.

He has endeavoured to prevent the population of these States; for that purpose obstructing the Laws of Naturalization of Foreigners; refusing to pass others to encourage their migrations hither, and raising the conditions of new Appropriations of Lands.

He has obstructed the Administration of Justice, by refusing his Assent to Laws for establishing Judiciary powers.

He has made Judges dependent on his Will alone, for the tenure of their offices, and the amount and payment of their salaries.

He has erected a multitude of New Offices, and sent hither swarms of Officers to harass our People, and eat out their substance.

He has kept among us, in times of peace, Standing Armies without the Consent of our legislatures.

He has affected to render the Military independent of and superior to the Civil power.

He has combined with others to subject us to a jurisdiction foreign to our constitution, and unacknowledged by by our laws; giving his Assent to their Acts of pretended Legislation.

For quartering large bodies of armed troops among us

For protecting them, by a mock Trial, from Punishment for any Murders which they should commit on the Inhabitants of these States

For cutting off our Trade with all parts of the world.

For imposing Taxes on us without our Consent.

For depriving us in many cases, of the benefits of Trial by Jury.

For transporting us beyond Seas to be tried for pretended offences.

For abolishing the free System of English Laws in a neighbouring Province, establishing therein an Arbitrary government, and enlarging its Boundaries so as to render it at once an example and fit instrument for introducing the same absolute rule into these Colonies.

For taking away our Charters, abolishing our most valuable Laws, and altering fundamentally the Forms of our Governments.

For suspending our own Legislatures, and declaring themselves invested with power to legislate for us in all cases whatsoever.

He has abdicated Government here, by declaring us out of his Protection and waging War against us.

He has plundered our seas, ravaged our Coasts, burnt our towns, and destroyed the Lives of our people.

He is at this time transporting large armies of foreign mercenaries to complete the works of death, desolation and tyranny, already begun with circumstances of Cruelty & perfidy scarcely paralleled in the most barbarous ages, and totally unworthy the Head of a civilized nation.

He has constrained our fellow Citizens taken Captive on the high Seas to bear Arms against their Country, to become the executioners of their friends and Brethren, or to fall themselves by their Hands.

He has excited domestic insurrections amongst us, and has endeavoured to bring on the inhabitants of our frontiers, the merciless Indian Savages, whose known rule of warfare, is an undistinguished destruction of all ages, sexes and conditions.

In every stage of these Oppressions We have Petitioned for Redress in the most humble terms: Our repeated Petitions have been answered only by repeated injury. A Prince, whose character is thus marked by every act which may define a Tyrant, is unfit to be the ruler of a free people.

Nor have We been wanting in attention to our British brethren.

We have warned them from time to time of attempts by their legislature to extend an unwarrantable jurisdiction over us.

We have reminded them of the circumstances of our emigration and settlement here. We have appealed to their native justice and magnanimity, and we have conjured them by the ties of our common kindred to disavow these usurpations, which would iinevitably interrupt our connections and correspondence. They too have been deaf to the voice of justice and of consanguinity. We must, therefore, acquiesce in the necessity, which denounces our Separation, and hold them, as we hold the rest of mankind, Enemies in War, in Peace Friends.

We, therefore, the Representatives of the united States of America, in General Congress, Assembled, appealing to the Supreme Judge of the world for the rectitude of our intentions, do, in the Name, and by Authority of the good People of these Colonies, solemnly publish and declare, That these United Colonies are, and of Right ought to be Free and Independent States; that they are Absolved from all Allegiance to the British Crown, and that all political connection between them and the State of Great Britain, is and ought to be totally dissolved; and that as Free and Independent States, they have full Power to levy War, conclude Peace, contract Alliances, establish Commerce, and to do all other Acts and Things which Independent States may of right do.

And for the support of this Declaration, with a firm reliance on the Protection of Divine Providence, we mutually pledge to each other our Lives, our Fortunes and our sacred Honor.

Appendix C

Constitution of the United States

We the People of the United States, in Order to form a more perfect Union, establish Justice, insure domestic Tranquility, provide for the common defence, promote the general Welfare, and secure the Blessings of Liberty to ourselves and our Posterity, do ordain and establish this Constitution for the United States of America.

Article I

Section 1. All legislative Powers herein granted shall be vested in a Congress of the United States, which shall consist of a Senate and House of Representatives.

Section 2. The House of Representatives shall be composed of Members chosen every second Year by the People of the several States, and the Electors in each State shall have the Qualifications requisite for Electors of the most numerous Branch of the State Legislature.

No Person shall be a Representative who shall not have attained to the age of twenty five Years, and been seven Years a Citizen of the United States, and who shall not, when elected, be an Inhabitant of that State in which he shall be chosen.

Representatives and direct Taxes shall be apportioned among the several States which may be included within this Union, according to their respective Numbers, which shall be determined by adding to the whole Number of free Persons, including those bound to Service for a Term of Years, and excluding Indians not taxed, three fifths of all other Persons. The actual Enumeration shall be made within three Years after the first Meeting of the Congress of the United States, and within every subsequent Term of ten Years, in such Manner as they shall by Law direct. The

Number of Representatives shall not exceed one for every thirty Thousand, but each State shall have at Least one Representative; and until such enumeration shall be made, the State of New Hampshire shall be entitled to chuse three, Massachusetts eight, Rhode-Island and Providence Plantations one, Connecticut five, New York six, New Jersey four, Pennsylvania eight, Delaware one, Maryland six, Virginia ten, North Carolina five, South Carolina five, and Georgia three.

When vacancies happen in the Representation from any State, the Executive Authority thereof shall issue Writs of Election to fill such Vacancies.

The House of Representatives shall chuse their Speaker and other Officers; and shall have the sole Power of Impeachment.

Section 3. The Senate of the United States shall be composed of two Senators from each State, chosen by the Legislature thereof, for six Years; and each Senator shall have one Vote.

Immediately after they shall be assembled in Consequence of the first Election, they shall be divided as equally as may be into three Classes. The Seats of the Senators of the first Class shall be vacated at the Expiration of the second Year, of the second Class at the Expiration of the fourth Year, and the third Class at the Expiration of the sixth Year, so that one third may be chosen every second Year; and if Vacancies happen by Resignation, or otherwise, during the Recess of the Legislature of any State, the Executive thereof may make temporary Appointments until the next Meeting of the Legislature, which shall then fill such Vacancies.

No Person shall be a Senator who shall not have attained to the Age of thirty Years, and been nine Years a Citizen of the United States and who shall not, when elected, be an Inhabitant of that State for which he shall be chosen.

The Vice President of the United States shall be President of the Senate, but shall have no Vote, unless they be equally divided.

The Senate shall chuse their other Officers, and also a President pro tempore, in the Absence of the Vice President, or when he shall exercise the Office of President of the United States.

The Senate shall have the sole Power to try all Impeachments. When sitting for that Purpose, they shall be on Oath or Affirmation. When the President of the United States is tried, the Chief Justice shall preside: And no Person shall be convicted without the Concurrence of two thirds of the Members present.

Judgment in Cases of Impeachment shall not extend further than to removal from Office, and disqualification to hold and enjoy any Office of Honor, Trust or Profit under the United States: but the Party convicted shall nevertheless be liable and subject to Indictment, Trial, Judgment and Punishment, according to Law.

Section 4. The Times, Places and Manner of holding Elections for Senators and Representatives, shall be prescribed in each State by the Legislature thereof; but the Congress may at any time by Law make or alter such Regulations, except as to the Places of chusing Senators.

The Congress shall assemble at least once in every Year, and such Meeting shall be on the first Monday in December, unless they shall by Law appoint a different Day.

Section 5. Each House shall be the Judge of the Elections, Returns and Qualifications of its own Members, and a Majority of each shall constitute a Quorum to do Business; but a smaller Number may adjourn from day to day, and may be authorized to compel the Attendance of absent Members, in such Manner, and under such Penalties as each House may provide.

Each House may determine the Rules of its Proceedings, punish its Members for disorderly Behaviour, and, with the Concurrence of two thirds, expel a Member.

Each House shall keep a Journal of its Proceedings, and from time to time publish the same, excepting such Parts as may in their Judgment require Secrecy; and the Yeas and Nays of the Members of either House on any question shall, at the Desire of one fifth of those Present, be entered on the Journal.

Neither House, during the Session of Congress, shall, without the Consent of the other, adjourn for more than three days, nor to any other Place than that in which the two Houses shall be sitting.

Section 6. The Senators and Representatives shall receive a Compensation for their Services, to be ascertained by Law, and paid out of the Treasury of the United States. They shall in all Cases, except Treason, Felony and Breach of the Peace, be privileged from Arrest during their Attendance at the Session of their respective Houses, and in going to and returning from the same; and for any Speech or Debate in either House, they shall not be questioned in any other Place.

No Senator or Representative shall, during the Time for which he was elected, be appointed to any civil Office under the Authority of the United States, which shall have been created, or the Emoluments whereof shall have been encreased during such time: and no Person holding any Office under the United States, shall be a Member of either House during his Continuance in Office.

Section 7. All Bills for raising Revenue shall originate in the House of Representatives; but the Senate may propose or concur with Amendments as on other Bills.

Every Bill which shall have passed the House of Representatives and the Senate, shall, before it become a Law, be presented to the President of the United States; if he approve he shall sign it, but if not he shall return it, with his

Objections to that House in which it shall have originated, who shall enter the Objections at large on their Journal, and proceed to reconsider it. If after such Reconsideration two thirds of that House shall agree to pass the Bill, it shall be sent, together with the Objections, to the other House, by which it shall likewise be reconsidered, and if approved by two thirds of that House, it shall become a Law. But in all such Cases the Votes of both Houses shall be determined by Yeas and Nays, and the Names of the Persons voting for and against the Bill shall be entered on the Journal of each House respectively. If any Bill shall not be returned by the President within ten Days (Sundays excepted) after it shall have been presented to him, the Same shall be a Law, in like Manner as if he had signed it, unless the Congress by their Adjournment prevent its Return, in which Case it shall not be a Law.

Every Order, Resolution, or Vote to which the Concurrence of the Senate and House of Representatives may be necessary (except on a question of Adjournment) shall be presented to the President of the United States; and before the Same shall take Effect, shall be approved by him, or being disapproved by him, shall be repassed by two thirds of the Senate and House of Representatives, according to the Rules and Limitations prescribed in the Case of a Bill.

Section 8. The Congress shall have Power To lay and collect Taxes, Duties, Imposts and Excises, to pay the Debts and provide for the common Defence and general Welfare of the United States; but all Duties, Imposts and Excises shall be uniform throughout the United States;

To borrow Money on the credit of the United States;

To regulate Commerce with foreign Nations, and among the several States, and with the Indian Tribes;

To establish an uniform Rule of Naturalization, and uniform Laws on the subject of Bankruptcies throughout the United States;

To coin Money, regulate the Value thereof, and of foreign Coin, and fix the Standard of Weights and Measures;

To provide for the Punishment of counterfeiting the Securities and current Coin of the United States;

To establish Post Offices and post Roads;

To promote the Progress of Science and useful Arts, by securing for limited Times to Authors and Inventors the exclusive Right to their respective Writings and Discoveries;

To constitute Tribunals inferior to the supreme Court;

To define and punish Piracies and Felonies committed on the high Seas, and Offences against the Law of Nations;

To declare War, grant Letters of Marque and Reprisal, and make Rules concerning Captures on Land and Water;

To raise and support Armies, but no Appropriation of Money to that Use shall be for a longer Term than two Years;

To provide and maintain a Navy;

To make Rules for the Government and Regulation of the land and naval Forces;

To provide for calling forth the Militia to execute the Laws of the Union, suppress Insurrections and repel Invasions;

To provide for organizing, arming, and disciplining, the Militia, and for governing such Part of them as may be employed in the Service of the United States, reserving to the States respectively, the Appointment of the Officers, and the Authority of training the Militia according to the discipline prescribed by Congress;

To exercise exclusive Legislation in all Cases whatsoever, over such District (not exceeding ten Miles square) as may, by Cession of particular States, and the Acceptance of Congress, become the Seat of the Government of the United States, and to exercise like Authority over all Places purchased by the Consent of the Legislature of the State in which the Same shall be, for the Erection of Forts, Magazines, Arsenals, dock-Yards, and other needful Buildings;--And

To make all Laws which shall be necessary and proper for carrying into Execution the foregoing Powers, and all other Powers vested by this Constitution in the Government of the United States, or in any Department or Officer thereof.

Section 9. The Migration or Importation of such Persons as any of the States now existing shall think proper to admit, shall not be prohibited by the Congress prior to the Year one thousand eight hundred and eight, but a Tax or duty may be imposed on such Importation, not exceeding ten dollars for each Person.

The Privilege of the Writ of Habeas Corpus shall not be suspended, unless when in Cases of Rebellion or Invasion the public Safety may require it.

No Bill of Attainder or ex post facto Law shall be passed.

No Capitation, or other direct, Tax shall be laid, unless in Proportion to the Census or Enumeration herein before directed to be taken.

No Tax or Duty shall be laid on Articles exported from any State.

No Preference shall be given by any Regulation of Commerce or Revenue to the Ports of one State over those of another: nor shall Vessels bound to, or from, one State, be obliged to enter, clear or pay Duties in another.

No Money shall be drawn from the Treasury, but in Consequence of Appropriations made by Law; and a regular Statement and Account of Receipts and Expenditures of all public Money shall be published from time to time.

No Title of Nobility shall be granted by the United States: And no Person holding any Office of Profit or Trust under them, shall, without the Consent of the Congress, accept of any present, Emolument, Office, or Title, of any kind whatever, from any King, Prince, or foreign State.

Section 10. No State shall enter into any Treaty, Alliance, or Confederation; grant Letters of Marque and Reprisal; coin Money; emit Bills of Credit; make any Thing but gold and silver Coin a Tender in Payment of Debts; pass any Bill of Attainder, ex post facto Law, or Law impairing the Obligation of Contracts, or grant any Title of Nobility.

No State shall, without the Consent of the Congress, lay any Imposts or Duties on Imports or Exports, except what may be absolutely necessary for executing it's inspection Laws: and the net Produce of all Duties and Imposts, laid by any State on Imports or Exports, shall be for the Use of the Treasury of the United States; and all such Laws shall be subject to the Revision and Controul of the Congress.

No State shall, without the Consent of Congress, lay any Duty of Tonnage, keep Troops, or Ships of War in time of Peace, enter into any Agreement or Compact with another State, or with a foreign Power, or engage in War, unless actually invaded, or in such imminent Danger as will not admit of delay.

Article II

Section 1. The executive Power shall be vested in a President of the United States of America. He shall hold his Office during the Term of four Years, and, together with the Vice President, chosen for the same Term, be elected, as follows:

Each State shall appoint, in such Manner as the Legislature thereof may direct, a Number of Electors, equal to the whole Number of Senators and Representatives to which the State may be entitled in the Congress: but no Senator or Representative, or Person holding an Office of Trust or Profit under the United States, shall be appointed an Elector.

The Electors shall meet in their respective States, and vote by Ballot for two Persons, of whom one at least shall not be an Inhabitant of the same State with themselves. And they shall make a List of all the Persons voted for, and of the Number of Votes for each; which List they shall sign and certify, and transmit sealed to the Seat of the Government of the United States, directed to the President of the Senate. The President of the Senate shall, in the Presence of the Senate and House of Representatives, open all the Certificates, and the Votes shall then be counted. The Person having the greatest Number of Votes shall be the President, if such Number be a Majority of the whole Number of Electors appointed; and if there be more than one who have such Majority, and have an equal Number of Votes, then the House of Representatives shall immediately chuse by Ballot one of them for President; and if no Person have a Majority, then from the five highest on the List the said House shall in like Manner chuse the President. But in chusing the President, the Votes shall be taken by States, the Representation from each State having one Vote; A quorum for this Purpose shall consist of a Member or Members from two thirds of the States, and a Majority of all the States shall be necessary to a Choice. In every Case, after the Choice of the President, the Person having the greatest Number of Votes of the Electors shall be the Vice President. But if there should remain two or more who have equal Votes, the Senate shall chuse from them by Ballot the Vice President.

The Congress may determine the Time of chusing the Electors, and the Day on which they shall give their Votes; which Day shall be the same throughout the United States.

No Person except a natural born Citizen, or a Citizen of the United States, at the time of the Adoption of this Constitution, shall be eligible to the Office of President; neither shall any Person be eligible to that Office who shall not have attained to the Age of thirty five Years, and been fourteen Years a Resident within the United States.

In Case of the Removal of the President from Office, or of his Death, Resignation, or Inability to discharge the

Powers and Duties of the said Office, the Same shall devolve on the Vice President, and the Congress may by Law provide for the Case of Removal, Death, Resignation or Inability, both of the President and Vice President, declaring what Officer shall then act as President, and such Officer shall act accordingly, until the Disability be removed, or a President shall be elected.

The President shall, at stated Times, receive for his Services, a Compensation, which shall neither be encreased nor diminished during the Period for which he shall have been elected, and he shall not receive within that Period any other Emolument from the United States, or any of them.

Before he enter on the Execution of his Office, he shall take the following Oath or Affirmation:--"I do solemnly swear (or affirm) that I will faithfully execute the Office of President of the United States, and will to the best of my Ability, preserve, protect and defend the Constitution of the United States."

Section 2. The President shall be Commander in Chief of the Army and Navy of the United States, and of the Militia of the several States, when called into the actual Service of the United States; he may require the Opinion, in writing, of the principal Officer in each of the executive Departments, upon any Subject relating to the Duties of their respective Offices, and he shall have Power to grant Reprieves and Pardons for Offences against the United States, except in Cases of Impeachment.

He shall have Power, by and with the Advice and Consent of the Senate, to make Treaties, provided two thirds of the Senators present concur; and he shall nominate, and by and with the Advice and Consent of the Senate, shall appoint Ambassadors, other public Ministers and Consuls, Judges of the supreme Court, and all other Officers of the United States, whose Appointments are not herein otherwise provided for, and which shall be established by Law: but the Congress may by Law vest the Appointment of such inferior Officers, as they think proper, in the President alone, in the Courts of Law, or in the Heads of Departments.

The President shall have Power to fill up all Vacancies that may happen during the Recess of the Senate, by granting Commissions which shall expire at the End of their next Session.

Section 3. He shall from time to time give to the Congress Information of the State of the Union, and recommend to their Consideration such Measures as he shall judge necessary and expedient; he may, on extraordinary Occasions, convene both Houses, or either of them, and in Case of Disagreement between them, with Respect to the Time of Adjournment, he may adjourn them to such Time as he shall think proper; he shall receive Ambassadors and other public Ministers; he shall take Care that the Laws be faithfully executed, and shall Commission all the Officers of the United States.

Section 4. The President, Vice President and all civil Officers of the United States, shall be removed from Office on Impeachment for, and Conviction of, Treason, Bribery, or other high Crimes and Misdemeanors.

Article III

Section 1. The judicial Power of the United States, shall be vested in one supreme Court, and in such inferior Courts as the Congress may from time to time ordain and establish. The Judges, both of the supreme and inferior Courts, shall hold their Offices during good Behaviour, and shall, at stated Times, receive for their Services, a Compensation, which shall not be diminished during their Continuance in Office.

Section 2. The judicial Power shall extend to all Cases, in Law and Equity, arising under this Constitution, the Laws of the United States, and Treaties made, or which shall be made, under their Authority;--to all Cases affecting Ambassadors, other public Ministers and Consuls;--to all Cases of admiralty and maritime Jurisdiction;--to Controversies to which the United States shall be a Party;--to Controversies between two or more States;--between a State and Citizens of another State;--between Citizens of different States;--between Citizens of the same State claiming Lands under Grants of different States, and between a State, or the Citizens thereof, and foreign States, Citizens or Subjects.

In all Cases affecting Ambassadors, other public Ministers and Consuls, and those in which a State shall be Party, the supreme Court shall have original Jurisdiction. In all the other Cases before mentioned, the supreme Court shall have appellate Jurisdiction, both as to Law and Fact, with such Exceptions, and under such Regulations as the Congress shall make.

The Trial of all Crimes, except in Cases of Impeachment, shall be by Jury; and such Trial shall be held in the State where the said Crimes shall have been committed; but when not committed within any State, the Trial shall be at such Place or Places as the Congress may by Law have directed.

Section 3. Treason against the United States, shall consist only in levying War against them, or in adhering to their Enemies, giving them Aid and Comfort. No Person shall be convicted of Treason unless on the Testimony of two Witnesses to the same overt Act, or on Confession in open Court.

The Congress shall have Power to declare the Punishment of Treason, but no Attainder of Treason shall work Corruption of Blood, or Forfeiture except during the Life of the Person attainted.

Article IV

Section 1. Full Faith and Credit shall be given in each State to the public Acts, Records, and judicial Proceedings of every other State. And the Congress may by general Laws prescribe the Manner in which such Acts, Records, and Proceedings shall be proved, and the Effect thereof.

Section 2. The Citizens of each State shall be entitled to all Privileges and Immunities of Citizens in the several States.

A Person charged in any State with Treason, Felony, or other Crime, who shall flee from Justice, and be found in another State, shall on Demand of the executive Authority of the State from which he fled, be delivered up, to be removed to the State having Jurisdiction of the Crime.

No Person held to Service or Labour in one State, under the Laws thereof, escaping into another, shall, in Consequence of any Law or Regulation therein, be discharged from such Service or Labour, but shall be delivered up on Claim of the Party to whom such Service or Labour may be due.

Section 3. New States may be admitted by the Congress into this Union; but no new States shall be formed or erected within the Jurisdiction of any other State; nor any State be formed by the Junction of two or more States, or Parts of States, without the Consent of the Legislatures of the States concerned as well as of the Congress.

The Congress shall have Power to dispose of and make all needful Rules and Regulations respecting the Territory or other Property belonging to the United States; and nothing in this Constitution shall be so construed as to Prejudice any Claims of the United States, or of any particular State.

Section 4. The United States shall guarantee to every State in this Union a Republican Form of Government, and shall protect each of them against Invasion; and on Application of the Legislature, or of the Executive (when the

Legislature cannot be convened) against domestic Violence.

Article V

The Congress, whenever two thirds of both Houses shall deem it necessary, shall propose Amendments to this Constitution, or, on the Application of the Legislatures of two thirds of the several States, shall call a Convention for proposing Amendments, which, in either Case, shall be valid to all Intents and Purposes, as Part of this Constitution, when ratified by the Legislatures of three fourths of the several States, or by Conventions in three fourths thereof, as the one or the other Mode of Ratification may be proposed by the Congress; Provided that no Amendment which may be made prior to the Year One thousand eight hundred and eight shall in any Manner affect the first and fourth Clauses in the Ninth Section of the first Article; and that no State, without its Consent, shall be deprived of its equal Suffrage in the Senate.

Article VI

All Debts contracted and Engagements entered into, before the Adoption of this Constitution, shall be as valid against the United States under this Constitution, as under the Confederation.

This Constitution, and the Laws of the United States which shall be made in Pursuance thereof; and all Treaties made, or which shall be made, under the Authority of the United States, shall be the supreme Law of the Land; and the Judges in every State shall be bound thereby, any Thing in the Constitution or Laws of any State to the Contrary notwith-standing.

The Senators and Representatives before mentioned, and the Members of the several State Legislatures, and all executive and judicial Officers, both of the United States and of the several States, shall be bound by Oath or Affirmation, to support this Constitution; but no religious Test shall ever be required as a Qualification to any Office or public Trust under the United States.

Article VII

The Ratification of the Conventions of nine States, shall be sufficient for the Establishment of this Constitution between the States so ratifying the Same.

Done in Convention by the Unanimous Consent of the States present the Seventeenth Day of September in the Year of our Lord one thousand seven hundred and Eighty seven and of the Independence of the United States of America the Twelfth

In witness whereof We have hereunto subscribed our Names,

George Washington--President and deputy from Virginia

New Hampshire: John Langdon, Nicholas Gilman

Massachusetts: Nathaniel Gorham, Rufus King

Connecticut: William Samuel Johnson, Roger Sherman

New York: Alexander Hamilton

New Jersey: William Livingston, David Brearly, William Paterson, Jonathan Dayton

Pennsylvania: Benjamin Franklin, Thomas Mifflin, Robert Morris, George Clymer, Thomas FitzSimons, Jared Ingersoll, James Wilson, Gouverneur Morris

Delaware: George Read, Gunning Bedford, Jr., John Dickinson, Richard Bassett, Jacob Broom

Maryland: James McHenry, Daniel of Saint Thomas Jenifer, Daniel Carroll

Virginia: John Blair, James Madison, Jr.

North Carolina: William Blount, Richard Dobbs Spaight, Hugh Williamson

South Carolina: John Rutledge, Charles Cotesworth Pinckney, Charles Pinckney, Pierce Butler

Georgia: William Few, Abraham Baldwin

AMENDMENTS TO THE CONSTITUTION OF THE UNITED STATES

Amendment I

Congress shall make no law respecting an establishment of religion, or prohibiting the free exercise thereof; or abridging the freedom of speech, or of the press; or the right of the people peaceably to assemble, and to petition the Government for a redress of grievances.

Amendment II

A well regulated Militia, being necessary to the security of a free State, the right of the people to keep and bear Arms, shall not be infringed.

Amendment III

No Soldier shall, in time of peace be quartered in any house, without the consent of the Owner, nor in time of war, but in a manner to be prescribed by law.

Amendment IV

The right of the people to be secure in their persons, houses, papers, and effects, against unreasonable searches and seizures, shall not be violated, and no Warrants shall issue, but upon probable cause, supported by Oath or affirmation, and particularly describing the place to be searched, and the persons or things to be seized.

Amendment V

No person shall be held to answer for a capital, or otherwise infamous crime, unless on a presentment or indictment of a Grand Jury, except in cases arising in the land or naval forces, or in the Militia, when in actual service in time of War or public danger; nor shall any person be subject for the same offence to be twice put in jeopardy of life or limb; nor shall be compelled in any criminal case to be a witness against himself, nor be deprived of life, liberty, or property, without due process of law; nor shall private property be taken for public use, without just compensation.

Amendment VI

In all criminal prosecutions, the accused shall enjoy the right to a speedy and public trial, by an impartial jury of the State and district wherein the crime shall have been committed, which district shall have been previously ascertained by law, and to be informed of the nature and cause of the accusation; to be confronted with the witnesses against him; to have compulsory process for obtaining witnesses in his favor, and to have the Assistance of Counsel for his defence.

Amendment VII

In Suits at common law, where the value in controversy shall exceed twenty dollars, the right of trial by jury shall be preserved, and no fact tried by a jury, shall be otherwise re-examined in any Court of the United States, than according to the rules of the common law.

Amendment VIII

Excessive bail shall not be required, nor excessive fines imposed, nor cruel and unusual punishments inflicted.

Amendment IX

The enumeration in the Constitution, of certain rights, shall not be construed to deny or disparage others retained by the people.

Amendment X

The powers not delegated to the United States by the Constitution, nor prohibited by it to the States, are reserved to the States respectively, or to the people.

Amendment XI

The Judicial power of the United States shall not be construed to extend to any suit in law or equity, commenced or prosecuted against one of the United States by Citizens of another State, or by Citizens or Subjects of any Foreign State.

Amendment XII

The Electors shall meet in their respective states and vote by ballot for President and Vice-President, one of whom, at least, shall not be an inhabitant of the same state with themselves; they shall name in their ballots the person voted for as President, and in distinct ballots the person voted for as Vice-President, and they shall make distinct lists of all persons voted for as President, and of all persons voted for as Vice-President, and of the number of votes for each, which lists they shall sign and certify, and transmit sealed to the seat of the government of the United States, directed to the President of the Senate;--The President of the Senate shall, in the presence of the Senate and House of Representatives, open all the certificates and the votes shall then be counted;--the person having the greatest number of votes for President, shall be the President, if such number be a majority of the whole number of Electors appointed; and if no person have such majority, then from the persons having the highest numbers not exceeding three on the list of those voted for as President, the House of Representatives shall choose immediately, by ballot, the President. But in choosing the President, the votes shall be taken by states, the representation from each state having one vote; a quorum for this purpose shall consist of a member or members from two-thirds of the states, and a majority of all the states shall be necessary to a choice. And if the House of Representatives shall not choose a President whenever the right of choice shall devolve upon them, before the fourth day of March next following, then the Vice-President shall act as President, as in the case of the death or other constitutional disability of the President.--The person having the greatest number of votes as Vice-President, shall be the Vice-President, if such number be a majority of the whole number of Electors appointed, and if no person have a majority, then from the two highest numbers on the list, the Senate shall choose the Vice-President; a quorum for the purpose shall consist of two-thirds of the whole number of Senators, and a majority of the whole number shall be necessary to a choice. But no person constitutionally ineligible to the office of President shall be eligible to that of Vice-President of the United States.

Amendment XIII

Section 1. Neither slavery nor involuntary servitude, except as a punishment for crime whereof the party shall have been duly convicted, shall exist within the United States, or any place subject to their jurisdiction.

Section 2. Congress shall have power to enforce this article by appropriate legislation.

Amendment XIV

Section 1. All persons born or naturalized in the United States, and subject to the jurisdiction thereof, are citizens of the United States and of the State wherein they reside. No State shall make or enforce any law which shall abridge the privileges or immunities of citizens of the United States; nor shall any State deprive any person of life, liberty, or property, without due process of law; nor deny to any person within its jurisdiction the equal protection of the laws.

Section 2. Representatives shall be apportioned among the several States according to their respective numbers, counting the whole number of persons in each State, excluding Indians not taxed. But when the right to vote at any election for the choice of electors for President and Vice President of the United States, Representatives in Congress, the Executive and Judicial officers of a State, or the members of the Legislature thereof, is denied to any of the male inhabitants of such State, being twenty-one years of age, and citizens of the United States, or in any way abridged, except for participation in rebellion, or other crime, the basis of representation therein shall be reduced in the proportion which the number of such male citizens shall bear to the whole number of male citizens twenty-one years of age in such State.

Section 3. No person shall be a Senator or Representative in Congress, or elector of President and Vice President, or hold any office, civil or military, under the United States, or under any State, who, having previously taken an oath, as a member of Congress, or as an officer of the United States, or as a member of any State legislature, or as an executive or judicial officer of any State, to support the Constitution of the United States, shall have engaged in insurrection or rebellion against the same, or given aid or comfort to the enemies thereof. But Congress may by a vote of two-thirds of each House, remove such disability.

Section 4. The validity of the public debt of the United States, authorized by law, including debts incurred for payment of pensions and bounties for services in suppressing insurrection or rebellion, shall not be questioned. But neither the United States nor any State shall assume or pay any debt or obligation incurred in aid of insurrection or rebellion against the United States, or any claim for the loss or emancipation of any slave; but all such debts, obligations and claims shall be held illegal and void.

Section 5. The Congress shall have power to enforce, by appropriate legislation, the provisions of this article.

Amendment XV

Section 1. The right of citizens of the United States to vote shall not be denied or abridged by the United States or by any State on account of race, color, or previous condition of servitude.

Section 2. The Congress shall have power to enforce this article by appropriate legislation.

Amendment XVI

The Congress shall have power to lay and collect taxes on incomes, from whatever source derived, without apportionment among the several States, and without regard to any census of enumeration.

Amendment XVII

The Senate of the United States shall be composed of two Senators from each State, elected by the people thereof, for six years; and each Senator shall have one vote. The electors in each State shall have the qualifications requisite for electors of the most numerous branch of the State legislatures.

When vacancies happen in the representation of any State in the Senate, the executive authority of such State shall issue writs of election to fill such vacancies: Provided, That the legislature of any State may empower the executive thereof to make temporary appointments until the people fill the vacancies by election as the legislature may direct.

This amendment shall not be so construed as to affect the election or term of any Senator chosen before it becomes valid as part of the Constitution.

Amendment XVIII

Section 1. After one year from the ratification of this article the manufacture, sale, or transportation of intoxicating liquors within, the importation thereof into, or the exportation thereof from the United States and all territory subject to the jurisdiction thereof for beverage purposes is hereby prohibited.

Section 2. The Congress and the several States shall have concurrent power to enforce this article by appropriate legislation.

Section 3. This article shall be inoperative unless it shall have been ratified as an amendment to the Constitution by the legislatures of the several States, as provided in the Constitution, within seven years from the date of the submission hereof to the States by the Congress.

Amendment XIX

The right of citizens of the United States to vote shall not be denied or abridged by the United States or by any State on account of sex.

Congress shall have power to enforce this article by appropriate legislation.

Amendment XX

Section 1. The terms of the President and Vice President shall end at noon on the 20th day of January, and the terms of Senators and Representatives at noon on the 3d day of January, of the years in which such terms would have ended if this article had not been ratified; and the terms of their successors shall then begin.

Section 2. The Congress shall assemble at least once in every year, and such meeting shall begin at noon on the 3d day of January, unless they shall by law appoint a different day.

Section 3. If, at the time fixed for the beginning of the term of the President, the President elect shall have died, the Vice President elect shall become President. If a President shall not have been chosen before the time fixed for the beginning of his term, or if the President elect shall have failed to qualify, then the Vice President elect shall act as President until a President shall have qualified; and the Congress may by law provide for the case wherein neither a President elect nor a Vice President elect shall have qualified, declaring who shall then act as President, or the manner in which one who is to act shall be selected, and such person shall act accordingly until a President or Vice President shall have qualified.

Section 4. The Congress may by law provide for the case of the death of any of the persons from whom the House of Representatives may choose a President whenever the right of choice shall have devolved upon them, and for the case of the death of any of the persons from whom the Senate may choose a Vice President whenever the right of choice shall have devolved upon them.

Section 5. Sections 1 and 2 shall take effect on the 15th day of October following the ratification of this article.

Section 6. This article shall be inoperative unless it shall have been ratified as an amendment to the Constitution by the legislatures of three-fourths of the several States within seven years from the date of its submission.

Amendment XXI

Section 1. The eighteenth article of amendment to the Constitution of the United States is hereby repealed.

Section 2. The transportation or importation into any State, Territory, or possession of the United States for delivery or use therein of intoxicating liquors, in violation of the laws thereof, is hereby prohibited.

Section 3. This article shall be inoperative unless it shall have been ratified as an amendment to the Constitution by conventions in the several States, as provided in the Constitution, within seven years from the date of the submission hereof to the States by the Congress.

Amendment XXII

Section 1. No person shall be elected to the office of the President more than twice, and no person who has held the office of President, or acted as President, for more than two years of a term to which some other person was elected President shall be elected to the office of the President more than once. But this Article shall not apply to any person holding the office of President when this Article was proposed by the Congress, and shall not prevent any person who may be holding the office of President, or acting as President, during the term within which this Article becomes operative from holding the office of President or acting as President during the remainder of such term.

Section 2. This article shall be inoperative unless it shall have been ratified as an amendment to the Constitution by the legislatures of three-fourths of the several States within seven years from the date of its submission to the States by the Congress.

Amendment XXIII

Section 1. The District constituting the seat of Government of the United States shall appoint in such manner as the Congress may direct:

A number of electors of President and Vice President equal to the whole number of Senators and Representatives in Congress to which the District would be entitled if it were a State, but in no event more than the least populous State; they shall be in addition to those appointed by the States, but they shall be considered, for the purposes of the election of President and Vice President, to be electors appointed by a State; and they shall meet in the District and perform such duties as provided by the twelfth article of amendment.

Section 2. The Congress shall have power to enforce this article by appropriate legislation.

Amendment XXIV

Section 1. The right of citizens of the United States to vote in any primary or other election for President or Vice President, for electors for President or Vice President, or for Senator or Representative in Congress, shall not be denied or abridged by the United States or any State by reason of failure to pay any poll tax or other tax.

Section 2. The Congress shall have power to enforce this article by appropriate legislation.

Amendment XXV

Section 1. In case of the removal of the President from office or of his death or resignation, the Vice President shall become President.

Section 2. Whenever there is a vacancy in the office of the Vice President, the President shall nominate a Vice President who shall take office upon confirmation by a majority vote of both Houses of Congress.

Section 3. Whenever the President transmits to the President pro tempore of the Senate and the Speaker of the House of Representatives his written declaration that he is unable to discharge the powers and duties of his office, and until he transmits to them a written declaration to the contrary, such powers and duties shall be discharged by the Vice President as Acting President.

Section 4. Whenever the Vice President and a majority of either the principal officers of the executive departments or of such other body as Congress may by law provide, transmit to the President pro tempore of the Senate and the Speaker of the House of Representatives their written declaration that the President is unable to discharge the powers and duties of his office, the Vice President shall immediately assume the powers and duties of the office as Acting President.

Thereafter, when the President transmits to the President pro tempore of the Senate and the Speaker of the House of Representatives his written declaration that no inability exists, he shall resume the powers and duties of his office unless the Vice President and a majority of either the principal officers of the executive department or of such other body as Congress may by law provide, transmit within four days to the President pro tempore of the Senate and the Speaker of the House of Representatives their written declaration that the President is unable to discharge the powers and duties of his office. Thereupon Congress shall decide the issue, assembling within forty-eight hours for that purpose if not in session. If the Congress, within twenty-one days after receipt of the latter written declaration, or, if Congress is not in session, within twenty-one days after Congress is required to assemble, determines by two-thirds vote of both Houses that the President is unable to discharge the powers and duties of his office, the Vice President shall continue to discharge the same as Acting President; otherwise, the President shall resume the powers and duties of his office.

Amendment XXVI

Section 1. The right of citizens of the United States, who are 18 years of age or older, to vote shall not be denied or abridged by the United States or any State on account of age.

Section 2. The Congress shall have the power to enforce this article by appropriate legislation.

Amendment XXVII

No law, varying the compensation for the service of the senators and representatives shall take effect, until an election of representatives shall have intervened.

Glossary

ad hoc A Latin phrase meaning "for this," that is, for a particular purpose. An ad hoc committee is one appointed for a particular purpose.

administrative law That branch of the law which deals with various agencies of the government, prescribing what they are supposed to do and how they are supposed to do it.

admiralty law That branch of the law that deals with maritime affairs, civil and criminal. Admiralty law is the law of the sea and is handled by the federal courts. It was handed down to the U.S. by Great Britain, which was primarily a maritime nation.

amnesty A general pardon granted by a government to all or certain persons guilty of an offense.

anarchy The absence of government; a condition of society having neither law nor supreme power.

antitrust acts Federal and state laws protecting commerce and trade from monopolies and illegal restraints.

appeal The taking of a case from a lower to a higher court for a review of the lower court's decision. An appeal is usually based on a claimed error of law by the lower court judge. In a civil case, either party can appeal; in a criminal case only the convicted defendant can appeal.

attorney in fact An agent to whom you give your power of attorney, as opposed to an attorney at law.

bicameral Consisting of two chambers, houses or branches; used to describe a legislative body, as in the US Congress.

bill of rights (1) A formal summary and declaration of the fundamental principles and rights of individuals, as for example the one enacted by the British Parliament in 1689; (2) The name given to the first ten amendments to the United States Constitution.

breach of the peace Unlawful disturbance of the public tranquillity, as by violent or disorderly behavior.

burden of proof The obligation to prove affirmatively a disputed fact or facts related to or bearing upon an issue that is raised between the parties in a case being tried before a court.

capital (1) The total amount of money or property owned or used by an individual or corporation. (2) The amount of property owned by an individual or corporation at a specified time, as distinct from the income received during a specified time. (3) Wealth in any form employed in or available for the production of more wealth or income. (4) Capital stock, that is, the amount of stock a corporation is authorized to issue; also, its total face value.

case law Law based on earlier decisions reached by the courts in similar situations, as opposed to written or statutory law.

charter (1) A formal document by which a sovereign or government grants special rights or privileges to a person or company or to the people. (2) A document of incorporation of a municipality, institution or corporation, specifying its privileges and purposes.

chattel An article of personal property.

civil action A lawsuit brought by a private individual or group to recover money or property, to enforce or protect a civil right, to prevent or redress a civil wrong. It differs from a criminal action in which the state prosecutes an individual for committing an offense against all the people.

codification The act or process of collecting and arranging the laws of a state or country into a systematically arranged, unified body called a code.

common law (1) In a wide sense, that system of law generally in force in a nation or state, as distinguished from regulations of local or specific application. (2) A system of jurisprudence based on custom, traditional usage and precedent, rather than on codified written laws; especially, the ancient unwritten law of England.

confiscate to appropriate for public use the private property that the owner has forfeited.

conflict of laws (1) The disagreement between the laws of different states or nations as it affects the rights of persons acting under the laws of more than one jurisdiction. (2) The branch of jurisprudence, sometimes called private international law, that determines which laws should be given effect or enforced in legal relations between citizens of different countries.

conspiracy In criminal law, a combination or agreement between two or more persons to commit an act punishable by law or to effect a legal purpose by criminal or unlawful means.

constitution (1) The organic law of any organized body or association. (2) The fundamental laws and principles (written or unwritten) that normally govern the operations of a nation or state; also, a document recording such laws and principles. (3) The Constitution of the United States, written and signed in 1787, went into effect March 4, 1789.

constitutional dictatorship Total authoritarian control by government during times of rebellion or invasion, in keeping with the US Constitution, Art.1 Sec. 9. As opposed to an unconstitutional dictatorship, which is total authoritarian control by government during times other than rebellion or invasion.

constitutional republic A union of sovereign nation states.

contract A legally enforceable agreement between two or more parties to do or not to do a particular thing, upon sufficient consideration.

corporate franchise The right granted by a government to a private corporation to exist and do business.

corporation An entity or artificial person created by law, consisting of one or more natural persons united in a body bearing a distinctive name. A corporation is endowed by the law with the capacity of perpetual succession - that is, it remains the same though its members may die or change - and is empowered to act as a unit or as a single individual.

court of last resort A tribunal from which there is no appeal.

court-martial A court of military or naval officers that is convened under the authority of the government and the Uniform Code of Military Justice to try offenses against military or naval law.

crime An act or omission in violation of a public law either forbidding or commanding it, for which a punishment is prescribed and which is prosecuted by the state in its own name or in the name of the people or the sovereign.

de facto A Latin expression meaning "in fact." It is often used to describe a government that has seized power by violent and unlawful means from a rightful, legally constituted government.

de jure A Latin expression meaning "by right" or "by law." It is used in reference to something, such as a corporation or government, that exists or functions in accordance with the law.

decree The decision of a court of equity, admiralty, divorce or probate. A decree corresponds to a judgment; the terms are often used synonymously.

deportation The sending back to the country from which he came of an alien whose presence is deemed incompatible with the public interest of the country sending him back.

desertion The willful abandonment, without legal justification or authority, of a person, obligation or post of duty.

disfranchise (1) To deprive a person of the rights and privileges of a free citizen, especially the right to vote. (2) To deprive (as a corporation) of a franchise, privilege or right.

dissent The disagreement of one or more judges on a court with the decision of a majority of judges in a case before that court. Such a disagreement is often set forth in a written opinion.

Doe, John A fictitious name used in a legal action to identify a party whose true name is unknown or who wishes to remain anonymous. Additional unknown or anonymous parties are sometimes known as Richard Roe and Peter Poe.

double jeopardy The subjection of a person to trial for the same offense that has already been tried under a valid charge. The Fifth Amendment to the Constitution protects citizens against double jeopardy.

due process of law A phrase used in reference to certain fundamental rights or principles of justice that limit the government's power to deprive a person of life, liberty or property. Its definition by Daniel Webster remains a classic. He said that due process denotes "law which hears before it condemns; which proceeds upon inquiry; and which renders judgment only after the trial."

emancipation The act of releasing from bondage, oppression or authority. (2) The surrender by a parent of authority and control over a minor child and also of the right to the child's earnings. An emancipated minor has certain rights that a minor does not usually have because of the legal independence of parental control.

embargo An order by a government restraining merchant vessels from leaving or entering its ports. Embargoes are often imposed in time of war or threatened hostilities, but are also used merely to control trade.

eminent domain The inherent sovereign power of the state to take private property for public use.

enjoin To direct, command, forbid or prohibit some act by court order.

entrapment The act of an officer of the government in inducing a person to commit a crime he had not contemplated so that the person may be prosecuted for the offense.

equal protection of law A phrase in the Fourteenth Amendment to the Constitution of the United States that requires that every state extend to all persons within its jurisdiction equal treatment and protection under the laws of that state. This guarantee applies both to privileges conferred and liabilities imposed. Unequal treatment is unconstitutional.

ex officio A Latin phrase meaning "from or by virtue of the office." For example, a corporate president is often an ex officio member of several committees of the corporation because of his position.

ex parte A Latin phrase meaning "from or in the interest of one side only." An ex parte order is an order granted by a court at the request of one party to a judicial proceeding without prior notification to the other party involved.

ex post facto A Latin phrase meaning "after the fact." An ex post facto law makes punishable as a crime, or increases the punishment for, an act that was not punishable at the time it was committed, or for which the penalty was then less severe.

excise tax (1) A tax imposed on certain commodities, as liquor and tobacco, that are produced, sold, used or transported within a country. (2) A tax imposed on licenses to pursue certain trades or occupations.

exempt To free or excuse from some obligation to which others are subjected, as, for example, military service, taxes, jury duty.

expatriation The voluntary giving up of citizenship in one's native country to take up citizenship in another.

extradition The surrender of a person accused or convicted of a crime by one government to the government having jurisdiction for the crime. Usually, extradition is arranged between sovereign states by means of treaties. Between the states of the United States, it is authorized under Article IV, Section 2, Clause 2, of the Constitution.

face amount The amount indicated by the actual language of an instrument, without taking into consideration any accrued interest, dividends, or discounts.

false arrest The unlawful restraint or detention of one person by another; any use or threat of force that makes someone stay where he does not want to stay or go where he does not want to go.

fine A sum of money required or paid as the penalty for an offense.

foreclosure Any one of several methods used in various states to enforce payment of a debt secured by a mortgage, by taking and selling the mortgaged property.

foreman A member of a grand or petit jury, appointed by the jury or by the court to speak for the jury, preside over its deliberations and communicate with the court.

franchise (1) Rights of a citizen, especially the right to vote. (2) A special privilege, such as the right to operate a bus line, granted an individual or corporation by the government. (3)Permission granted by an individual or corporation to sell a product or service under conditions set forth in the contract.

full faith and credit A phrase from the United States Constitution, Article IV, Section 1, which provides that "Full faith and credit shall be given in each State to the public acts, records, and judicial proceedings of every other State."

goods and chattels A general term denoting personal property as distinguished from real property.

grand jury A jury of from six to 23 persons called to hear complaints and accusations of the commission of crimes, to hear evidence produced by the state and to file indictments when the jury believes from such evidence that a crime has been committed.

habeas corpus A Latin phrase meaning "you have the body." The name of a number of writs designed to compel the bringing of the "body" or person before a court or judge; especially the *writ of habeas corpus ad subjiciendum* (Latin for "you should have the body for submitting") which directs the person having another in custody to produce the person detained as a means to enable the court to review the legality of his detention.

imminent danger A term used in reference to self-defense. It denotes danger of such immediacy that it must be instantly met and cannot wait upon the assistance of others or the protection of the law.

immunity Freedom from duty or penalty; exemption, as from tax.

impeach (1) Charge a public official before a legally constituted tribunal with crime in office. (2) Discredit or question the veracity of a witness. (3) Challenge the authenticity or accuracy of a document, decree, judgment or something of similar nature.

implied Intended but not directly or explicitly stated; deduced from circumstances, conduct or language; suggested or understood: contrasted with "express."

inalienable Not capable of being bought, sold, transferred, or taken away.

incite urge on to some action; stir up; instigate; more specifically, in criminal law, to urge or instigate another to commit a crime. In this sense, to abet.

indemnify (1) Compensate for loss or damage that has already occurred. (2) Give security against future loss or damage.

indictment A formal written charge of crime presented by a grand jury on oath to the court in which it is impaneled, as the basis for trial of the accused. The indictment is usually prepared by the prosecuting attorney for the government.

infringement Any breaking in upon, or violation of, a right, privilege, regulation, law or contract; used particularly in reference to the violation of rights secured by copyrights, patents and trademarks.

inheritance tax A tax on the passing of property, not on the property itself, by descent or will.

injunction An order, writ or process issued by a court of equity directing the person named therein to take, or more commonly, to refrain from taking, some specified action.

insurrection A revolt of citizens or subjects against their government.

intent The state of mind in which, or the purpose with which, one acts.

interim For or during an intervening period of time; in the meantime. A temporary injunction, for example, is an interim order.

international law The system of laws that regulates the relations among nations.

ipso facto A Latin phrase meaning "by the fact itself" or "by the mere effect of an act or fact."

jeopardy The danger of conviction or punishment in which a person is put when he is placed on trial upon a valid indictment before a competent court and a jury duly sworn.

judiciary (1) The branch of government in which judicial power is concentrated. (2) The system of courts set up to administer the law. (3) The judges of the courts considered as a body.

jurisdiction A comprehensive term, widely used to denote the legal right by which courts and judicial officers exercise their authority; the right or authority by which courts and judicial officers interpret and administer the law, whether in a general sense or in respect to some particular matter. It may refer to (a) the power of a court to render judgment against a specific person (b) the power of a court to hear and determine a particular type of action, or (c) the power to determine the rights of a person regarding property or a status or relation.

jurisprudence The science or philosophy of law, treating the principles of positive law and legal relations.

jury A body of qualified men and women (usually 12) selected and sworn in by a local court to try and determine any question of fact, in any civil or criminal proceeding, according to the law and the evidence given.

law (1) A rule of conduct, recognized by custom or decreed by formal enactment. (2) A body of such rules, considered by men or nations as binding and enforced in any given community by courts, administrative agencies or some authorized official. (3) The profession of a lawyer, attorney, counsel; the legal profession.

legislation (1) The act or procedures of making and enacting laws. (2) An officially enacted law or laws.

legitimate In accordance with law; authorized or sanctioned by law; lawful; legal.

levy (1) Impose or collect; exact, as a tax or fine. (2) Collect money by the seizure of property in satisfaction of a legal claim or judgment.

lex The Latin word for "law," used often in combination with other Latin words to denote a particular kind of law.

license (1) Permission granted by an authorized official to perform some act or engage in some business activity. (2) The document that grants such permission. (3) Written authorization by the owner of a patent empowering another person to make or use the patented article or process for a limited period of time in a limited area.

litigation A judicial contest; lawsuit.

magistrate A judge of a court of limited jurisdiction, as a justice of the peace or a judge in a police court.

malum in se A wrong in itself; an act that is wrong or evil by its very nature, whether or not it is punishable by law, as opposed to malum prohibitum.

malum prohibitum An act that is prohibited by law even though it may not be inherently wrong or immoral, as opposed to malum in se.

maritime law That system of laws pertaining to commerce and navigation on the high seas, harbors and coastal waters.

martial law Temporary jurisdiction or rule by military forces in an area where civil law and order do not exist or have broken down. It is really no law, because it suspends existing laws and procedures for administering justice.

military law The branch of law that concerns military discipline and the government of persons employed in the armed forces. Not to be confused with martial law.

militia A body of citizens enrolled and trained in military organizations other than the regular military forces and called out only in emergencies.

monopoly The exclusive right or power to carry on trade or a business, manufacture a product or control the total sale of a particular commodity. Such right (or power) is vested in one or more persons or companies by privilege (as a government grant) or peculiar advantage (as a corner on a market).

municipal (1) Of or pertaining to a town or city; more generally, pertaining to any local governmental unit. (2) Of or pertaining to the internal government of a state or nation.

mutiny A revolt by members of the armed forces against their commanders, or by merchant seamen against their captain.

negotiable instrument A check, note, bill of exchange or any other written security that can be transferred by endorsement and delivery, or by delivery only, which gives to the person to whom it is transferred the legal ownership, enabling him to demand the full amount called for on the face of the instrument.

neutrality The status of a nation that does not interfere or side with any belligerent in a war.

oath A solemn affirmation by which an individual certifies that he is bound in conscience to do something in good faith. An oath often contains an appeal to a personage or object regarded by the person swearing as high or holy, to witness the truth of the affirmation.

offense A breach of law, used to refer to both crimes and misdemeanors.

office (1) A position of trust and authority in government or business. (2) A legal right to exercise a public function or employment and to receive compensation.

opinion A formal statement by a judge or court; the decision reached in a case tried or argued before him. An opinion is an expression of the reasons and principles upon which such a decision has been based.

ordinance A law or statute; specially, an enactment of the lawmaking body of a municipal corporation.

owner A person who has the legal or rightful title to property.

pardon To release or excuse a person who has committed a crime from the entire punishment for the crime, even after conviction or before indictment or trial.

per capita A Latin phrase meaning "by heads; for each person; share and share alike." It is often used in the law of wills and descent and distribution to denote a method of dividing an estate by giving an equal share to each of a number of persons.

per se A Latin phrase meaning "by itself; intrinsically, inherently."

petit jury The jury that sits at a trial in civil and criminal cases.

petition A formal application in writing made to a court requesting judicial action concerning the matter set forth in the application.

piracy (1) Robbery on the high seas. (2) The unauthorized publication, reproduction, or use of another's copyrighted artistic work.

plaintiff The person who begins an action at law; the complaining party in an action.

police (1) That department of government whose responsibility it is to maintain order, promote safety, enforce the law and prevent and detect crime. (2) The members of such a department.

police power the power of government to make and enforce all laws and regulations deemed necessary for the good and welfare of the state and its citizens.

poll a jury To examine all the members of a jury individually to determine whether or not they have assented, and still do assent, to the verdict.

poll tax A tax on a person as distinguished from a tax on property, especially a prerequisite for voting.

preamble An introductory clause in a constitution, statute or resolution, explaining its intent and the reason for its adoption.

precedent An adjudged case or judicial decision that furnishes a rule or model for deciding a subsequent case that presents the same or a similar legal problem.

preliminary hearing The hearing given by a judge or magistrate to an accused person to determine whether or not there is sufficient evidence to require the commitment and holding to bail of the accused.

prerogative An exclusive and unquestionable right belonging to a person or body of persons.

presentment A statement made by a grand jury concerning some wrongdoing, based on the jury's own investigation and knowledge and presented in the court but not accompanied by an indictment.

presumption of law An inference based on the rule of law that courts and judges are compelled to draw a particular inference from a particular fact or from particular evidence, unless and until contrary evidence is offered that disproves the truth of such inference.

prima facie A Latin phrase meaning "at first view; on first appearance."Something that is assumed to be true or factual in the absence of evidence to the contrary. A prima facie case is a case strong enough that it can be overthrown only by contradicting or rebutting evidence. Prima facie evidence is evidence that, if unexplained or uncontradicted, would establish the fact alleged.

privacy, right of The right of an individual (or corporation) to be let alone, free from pubic scrutiny and unwarranted publicity.

privilege (1) A particular benefit, favor or advantage not enjoyed by all or enjoyed only under special conditions. (2) An exemption, resulting from one's office or position, from a burden or liability to which others are subject.

prize In admiralty law, property, such as a vessel and its cargo, captured at sea by a belligerent in conformity with the laws of war.

pro forma A Latin expression meaning "as a matter of form," used in relation to certain decisions rendered to facilitate other proceedings.

proclamation (1) A formal declaration. (2) Something formally spoken or written, especially a matter of great public interest made known by an authoritative official.

prohibition The name of a writ issued by a superior court commanding an inferior court to desist from proceeding in a matter not within its jurisdiction.

promissory note A written promise by one person to pay, unconditionally, to another person named therein, or to his order or to the bearer, a certain sum of money at a specified time or on demand.

property (1) The legal right to the possession, use, enjoyment and disposal of a thing; an unrestricted and exclusive right or interest in or to a thing. (2) Anything that may be owned or possessed.

prosecute Institute and carry forward an action or other judicial proceeding.

prosecutor (1) A person responsible to institute and carry forward a suit, especially a criminal suit, against another person in a court of justice. (2) A public officer that conducts criminal proceedings on behalf of the state or the public.

protest (1) A formal declaration of dissent by a person, who has done or is about to do some act, made to prevent the inference that by such act the protester has relinquished a right or accepted a liability. (2) A formal notarial certificate attesting the fact that a note or bill of exchange has been presented for acceptance or for payment and that it has been refused. (3) A formal statement in writing made by a person called upon to pay a sum of money, as an import duty or a tax, in which he declares that he does not concede the legality of the claim.

proviso A stipulation or clause, as in a contract or statute, limiting, modifying or rendering conditional its operation.

quasi Appearing as if; simulating in appearance; often used in combination with English words to suggest a lack of reality. A quasi corporation, for example, is a body that exercises certain corporate functions but is not expressly incorporated by statute.

quid pro quo A Latin phrase meaning "something for something," used to describe the consideration that passes between parties to a contract, rendering it valid and binding.

quorum The number of members of any deliberative or corporate body necessary for the legal transaction of business; a majority of the body.

ratification (1) The act of approving, confirming or sanctioning. (2) The acceptance or adoption of whatever has been done by another acting as representative or agent, especially where the other did not have original authority.

referendum The submission of a proposed public measure or law, which has been passed upon by a legislature or convention, to a vote of the people for ratification or rejection.

renunciation The act of surrendering or disclaiming a right or privilege without transferring it to another.

reprisal The forcible seizure of something from an enemy by way of retaliation or indemnity.

res judica A Latin phrase meaning "a matter decided," used in reference to an issue or point of law that has been previously decided in respect to the parties involved by a court of authoritative or competent jurisdiction. Once decided, the point is not to be decided again.

rescind Make void; abrogate; annul; cancel; especially to abrogate a contract from its beginning, restoring the parties to the positions they occupied before the contract was made; restitution (1) Restoration of the parties to a rescinded contract to the positions they occupied before making the contract. (2)Restoration of property to the person entitled to it after the reversal of a judgment under which the property was taken.

restraint of trade Agreements or understandings between companies that are designed to stifle competition, fix prices or otherwise obstruct the natural course of commercial and business activity.

retroactive law A law that relates to and affects actions that occurred before the law came into effect. See also ex post facto.

reverse To annul, vacate, set aside or revoke, as a judgment order.

revocation Annulment; cancellation; repeal; reversal; rescission.

riot A tumultuous disturbance of the public peace by three or more assembled persons in a manner calculated to terrorize the people.

sabotage The malicious damaging of property or a deliberate slowdown of work, either to interfere with or to halt industrial production.

sanction The penalty or punishment for violating a law.

search and seizure The examination of a person's premises or of his person in an effort to find stolen or illicit property or contraband, or to discover evidence of his guilt that may be used in prosecuting a crime with which the person is charged.

search warrant A judicial order in writing, directing an officer to search a house or other specified place for things, alleged to be unlawfully concealed there.

sedition Conduct or language directed against public order and the tranquillity of the state; disorder or commotion in a state, not reaching the point of insurrection; also, the stirring up of such disorder, tending toward treason but lacking an overt act.

seizure The act of forcibly taking real or personal property into legal possession.

self-defense The defense (or the right to such defense) of oneself or one's family from personal assault or of one's property from destructive violence.

separate but equal A phrase that denotes the doctrine used to justify separation of the white and black races, as in public schools or public transportation where segregated accommodations and facilities are supposed to be equal.

service of process The legal communication of a judicial process to the designated person. Such communication may be made by personal or constructive service. Personal service is made by personally delivering a copy of the process to the person concerned. Constructive service is made by sending the process through the mails, delivering it to an authorized representative or publishing it in a newspaper.

sheriff The chief administrative officer of a county, charged with executive duties in criminal courts and civil courts of record.

sine qua non A Latin phrase meaning "without which not" used to describe a thing or a condition that is essential or indispensable.

sinecure An office or position for which compensation is received but which involves few or no duties.

slander An oral statement of a false, malicious or defamatory nature, tending to damage another's reputation or means of livelihood.

solvency The condition of being able to pay all debts or just claims of one's creditors.

sovereign immunity The immunity of a government from being sued in its own courts except with its consent.

star chamber (1) Formerly, in England, a secret court held by members of the Privy Council with judges of the courts of common law and no jury. It was abolished by Parliament in 1641 because of abuses. (2) Any court engaged in arbitrary or illegal procedures.

stare decisis A Latin phrase meaning "to stand by decided matters." It refers to the judicial policy of following legal principles established by previous court decisions.

state's evidence The evidence of an accomplice or participant in a crime, tending to incriminate others and given in the hope of pardon or a lighter sentence.

states' rights Those rights and powers not delegated to the federal government by the United States Constitution nor prohibited by it to the respective states.

status quo The condition of a person or thing that is or has been; the existing situation at any given time.

statute A legislative body's written enactment, expressed in the form necessary to make it the law of the governmental unit concerned.

statutory law Law based on written laws or acts with exact words as drafted and approved by a federal, state or local legislature.

stay A stopping or suspension of judicial proceedings or the execution of a judgment.

steal To commit a theft; to unlawfully take away another person's property without the owner's consent, secretly and without the use of threat or violence.

subpoena A writ commanding a person to appear in court to give testimony.

subsidy Financial aid granted by the government to an individual or private enterprise deemed beneficial to the public.

suffrage The right or privilege of voting.

sui juris (1) Having the legal capacity to act for oneself. (2) Having full social and civil rights.

summary Immediate; speedily effected without ceremony or delay. In summary proceeding certain minor causes are handled by a judge without jury and without adherence to conventional trial procedure.

supreme court (1) In the United States and in various states, a court of appellate jurisdiction and, in most cases, of last resort. (2) In some states, such as New York, the highest trial court of general jurisdiction though not of last resort.

tariff (1) A list or schedule of merchandise with the rates of duty to be paid to the government upon their importation into the United States. (2) A duty levied according to such a schedule. (3) Any list or schedule of charges.

tax sale The sale of a delinquent taxpayer's property to collect payment of a tax due from the owner.

tenancy (1) The holding or possession of lands or buildings by any kind of right or title; for example, the temporary occupancy of a house or property under the terms of a lease. (2) The period during which a tenant holds or possesses land or a building.

tender A person's formal offer, of money or property, in satisfaction of some claim or demand held against him.

tenure (1) The fact or manner or term of holding or occupying some particular office. (2) Permanent status granted to an employee after a specified trial period of employment.

title (1) The right to or ownership of property. (2) The grounds whereby the owner of lands has the just possession of them.(3) The union of those elements that constitute legal ownership, divided at common law into possession, the right of possession and the right of property (the last two being to all intents and purposes interchangeable terms). (4) The legal evidence of a person's right of property; also, the means by which or the source from which a person has accrued his right of property.

treason An overt attempt to overthrow the government to which one owes allegiance.

treaty A formal agreement, league or contract, duly concluded and ratified between two or more nations or sovereigns.

trespass (1) Broadly, any voluntary transgression of law or rule of duty; any offense done to another's person or property. (2) More specifically, any unlawful act accompanied by force, either actual or implied, such as unauthorized entry on another person's land either intentionally or unintentionally.

trial The judicial examination of the issues, whether of law or of fact, between the parties to a civil or criminal action, such examination being conducted by a competent tribunal (either a judge alone or a judge and jury) in accordance with the law of the land.

tribunal (1) Court of justice (2) The seat, bench, or place set apart for judges.

tyranny Absolute power arbitrarily or unjustly administered; the exercise of sovereignty in a manner contrary to law or justice; despotism.

unconstitutional Contrary to or in violation of a constitution and therefore void and legally inoperative.

unconstituional dictatorship Total authoritarian control by government during times other than rebellion or enemy invasion.

uniform laws Laws approved by the National Conference of Commissioners on Uniform State Laws and adopted by one or more jurisdictions in the United

States and its possessions. Their aim is to make laws consistent from state to state.

union An association, as of persons, parties, states or nations, combined for some mutual interest or purpose.

unlawful assembly The coming together of three or more persons with a mutual intent to assist one another in the execution of some unlawful act using force and violence.

unlawful detainer The unlawful retention of possession of real property by a person, whose right to such possession has terminated and who refuses to quit the property.

usage A customary or habitual practice that is lawful, reasonable and either known to the involved parties or so well established that it is presumed that the parties have acted in accordance with it: evidence of an existing standard of practice.

voir dire A preliminary examination of a person, especially of a proposed witness or juror, as to his qualifications for the function or duty in question.

waiver (1) The voluntary relinquishment or abandonment of a right, privilege, claim or advantage, as in a waiver of immunity. (2) The instrument that evidences such relinquishment.

without prejudice Describing a judicial determination that in no way harms or cancels the legal rights or privileges of the parties concerned except as expressly stated. If a case is dismissed without prejudice, the plaintiff can bring suit again on the same cause of action.

without recourse Describing an endorsement of a negotiable instrument by which the endorser merely passes it on but accepts no liability to subsequent holders for its payment.

writ A written order issued by a court, commanding the person to whom it is addressed to do or not to do some act specified therein.

Bibliography

Congressional Record, August 15, 1921, Senate

Congressional Record, March 9, 1933, House and Senate

Grolier Multimedia Encyclopedia Release 6, Grolier Electronic Publishing, Inc., 1994

Public Papers of the Presidents of the U.S. - Herbert Hoover., U.S. Government Printing Office, Washington D.C., 1977

Senate Document No. 78, 65th Congress 1st Session. Present Dangers Confronting Our Country, U.S. Government Printing Office, Washington D.C., 1917

Senate Report 93-549, 93rd Congress 1st Session, Emergency Power Statutes, U.S. Government Printing Office, Washington D.C., 1973

Senate Report No. 113, 65th Congress 1st Session, Calendar No. 115. An Act to Define, Regulate, and Punish Trading with the Enemy, and for other Purposes.

Statutes

48 Stat. 1

48 Stat. 1 sec. 2(b)

48 Stat. 195 sec. 1

48 Stat. 195 sec. 2

48 Stat. 2 sec. 4

48 Stat. 20 sec. 404

48 Stat. 22-23

48 Stat. 39 sec. 13

48 Stat. 51 sec. 43

48 Stat. 60 sec. 2 (n)

48 Stat. 68 sec. 20,

48 Stat. 95 sec. 211

90 Stat. 1255

The Law of Civil Government in Territory Subject to Military Occupation by the Military Forces of the United States, U.S. Government Printing Office, Washington D.C., 1902

The Public Papers and Addresses of Franklin D. Roosevelt, Vol 1 - 7, Random House, New York, 1938

Adler, Mortimer J., *We Hold These Truths,* Macmillan, NY, 1987

Bartlett, Donald and Steele, James R., *America: What Went Wrong?*, Andrews and McMeel, Kansas City, 1992

Bordahl, Clarence A., PhD, *War Powers of the Executive in the United States,* Johnson Reprint Corp., 1921

Catton, Bruce, *Picture History of the Civil War,* Crown Publishers, NY, 1982

Clark, J. Ruben Jr., *Emergency Legislation Passed Prior to Dec., 1917 Dealing with the Control and Taking of Private Property Use, Benefit, or Welfare. Presidential Proclamations and Executive Orders Thereunder*, U.S. Government Printing Office, Washington D.C., 1918

Cooley, Thomas A., LLD, *The General Principles of Constitutional Law in the United States of America*, Little Brown Company, Boston, 1898

Copeland, Lewis and Lamm, Lawrence W., *The World's Greatest Speeches*, Dover, NY, 1973

Gross, Martin L., *A Call for Revolution,* Ballantine, NY, 1993

Higham, Charles, *Trading with the Enemy*, Delacorte Press, New York, 1983

Jaikaran, Jacques S., M.D., *Debt Virus*, Glenbridge Publishing Ltd., 1992

Kent, James, *Commentaries on American Law*, O. Halsted, New York, 0000

Poor, Henry V., *You and the Law,* Readers Digest, Pleasantville, NY, 1977

Rossiter, Clinton, *Constitutional Dictatorship: Crisis Government in the Modern Democracies*, Princeton University Press, Princeton, 1948

Schlesinger, Arthur M. Sr., *The Coming of the New Deal,* Houghton Mifflin Co., Boston, 1959

Story, Joseph, *Commenatries on the Constitution of the United States,* Hilliard Gray and Company, Cambridge, 1833

Supreme Court Decision, *Schecter Poultry Co. v. U. S.;* 295 U.S. 495 (1935)

Supreme Court Decision, *State of Georgia v. Stanton,* Supreme Court December Term 1867

Supreme Court Decision, *Stoehr v. Wallace* 255 U.S. 694 (1921)

Supreme Court Decision, *U. S. v. Butler,* 297 U.S. 1 (1936)

Swisher, Carl Brent, *Constitutional Development*, Riverside Press, Cambridge, 1943

Whiting, William, *War Powers Under the Constitution of the United States*, Reprinted Rio Grande Press Inc.,1971

Index

Does not include Appendix A, B, or C

10th Amendment
  forbids congress to delegate power 135
14th Amendment
  as war measure 170
  precedents set by 132
  ratification reqd for statehood 132, 169
16th Amendment
  establishing income tax 170
1928, conditions in 137
1929, collapse in 171

A

abrogation of gold clause
  Supreme Court says not valid . . . 58
Acheson, Dean
  North. invading .South Korea . . . 143
Adams, John 168
Afghanistan
  Soviet invasion of 155
Agent Orange 148
Agnew, Vice President Spiro T.
  resigns after accepting bribe . . . 153
Agricultural Adjustment Act . . . 36, 70
  gives pres. power over money .25, 37,47
  makes permanent agency 38
  ruled unconstitutional 60
  termination date left to president . . 47
  used to prop up value of assets . . . 38
agricultural credits 46
agriculture
  as national public interest 38
  supporting new money and credit . 46
  control of by government 46, 97
  permanent state of rule over . . . 106
Air Associates Incorporated 91
Alabama secedes from union . . . 123
Alien and Sedition Act 168
  pattern for Trading with Enemy Act 171
Allende, Salvadore 156
Alliance for Progress 145
America
  as group of trading companies . . . 11
  used to further British Dominion . . 11
American citizens
  placed in US concentration camps . 87
American Newspaper Guild 85
American people
  defined as enemy 31
  not enemies in original act 30
  included as enemies in amended . 31
  made subject to total war powers . 31
  treated as enemy 172
American troops
  aiding allies during neutrality 91
Anacostia, veterans camp at . . . 139
anti federalists 168
anti slavery societies
  in North and South 119
anti trust laws 88
  exempt trade organizations 49
  exemptions bought with licenses . 48
  to combat monopoly 48
armies
  standing, in time of peace 13
  without consent of legislatures . . . 13
arms, right to keep and bear 23
arms control talks
  frozen by Soviets 159
arms sales to Iran 160
Article 1 129
Article 48, Germany's
  as base of Hitler's dictatorship . . 114
  dictatorship article in Germany . 114
  use of by Chancellor Bruning . . 115
Article Eight 18
Article Five 17
Article Four 17
Article Nine 18
Article One 16
Article Seven 18
Article Six 18
Article Ten 18
Article Thirteen 19
Article Three 17
Article Two 17
assassination plot
  by CIA on Fidel Castro 156
assassinations attempted by CIA . 156
assets, control of 177
assets of allies
  protected by executive order . . . 92

Atlantic Conference and Charter . . . 91
Austria, German invasion of 89

B

bail, excessive 18, 21
balance of powers 178
bank accounts
  confiscation of 21
Bank Conservation Act 73
  See also Emergency Banking Act
  passed without reading bill 27
bank deposits
  guarantee of by FDIC 36
bank holiday proclaimed by FDR . . 26
bank robbery
  interstate commerce clause 76
bankers resolution
  cancelling of depositors contracts . 29
  claiming gold hoarding 29
  implemented by FDR 28
  fines for gold withdrawal 29
banking system
  control over by government 34
  established during great depression 25
banks
  bailout of 25, 36
  closing of 172
  exempted from law 172
  government investment in 85
  run on 172
  shortfall to pay back deposits . . . 34
Baruch, Bernard 136
Bay of Pigs invasion
  formulated by CIA 144
  under Kennedy 145
Bengh az i 159
Bennett, Senator
  on export controls 100
Berlin, division of 141
Big Brother 21
bill of rights
  and federal citizens 132
  to reinforce individual rights 16
Bituminous Coal Conservation Act
  ruled unconstitutional 62
Black Thursday 138
blacklisting
  countries aiding Italy and Germany 92
Blue Eagle
  used as sign of compliance 52
bombing of Iraq 162
bondage of American people 175
Bordahl, Clarence A. 171
borrowing
  to meet government expenses . . 33
Brandeis, Justice
  on tortured Constitution 61
Bretton Woods Agreement 44
British
  arbitrary rules against colonists . . 12
  need to finance war 12
  shows of force against colonies . . 12
Britten, Congressman 173
  Fed Res bank notes and mortgages 35
Brooks, Senator Preston
  canes colleague to insensibility . . 122
Brown, John
  seizure of Harpers Ferry 122
Bruning, Chancellor Heinrich
  use of emergency powers 115
budget message, annual, of 1934 . . 40
budgets, two operating 40
bureacracies
  created by Roosevelt 83
Bureau of Industrial Economics . . . 88
Bush, President George
  congress OK of war not needed 96, 162
  difficulty on logic of invading Iraq . 162
  grain embargo 107
  invasion of Panama, Kuwait 162
  personal notes on 163
  troops to Somalia 163
Butz, Secretary of Agriculture
  disincentives in farm pricing 102
  on farm price manipulation . . 100 103

C

Calhoun, James C. 120
Cambodia
  US bombing of 149, 151
Canada
  US aid to during neutrality 91
Captured Property Act of 1863 . . . 130
Cardozo, Justice
  tortured construction of Constitution 61
  opinion on NIRA 57
carpetbaggers 130, 170

Carter v Carter Coal Co. 63
Carter, President Jimmy
grain embargo 107
not part of establishment 156
personal notes on 157
problems during presidency . . . 155
Casey, CIA director William 160
Castro, Fidel 156
CIA plot against 144
censorship of press
said necessary for recovery 82
census bureau
established by executive order . . 68
chattel property
people as assets of government . . 43
cheap food policy 107
chemical warfare in Vietnam . . . 148
chemical weapons
suspected of in Libya 160
Child Protective Services 21
China 89
Churchill, Winston
personal notes on 118
use of emergency powers 117
CIA
attempt to overthrow Sandanistas 159
Carter orders activities curtailed . 156
plot against Fidel Castro 144
citizens
arbitrary rule over 5
as pawns 178
as ruling class 1
as subjects of government 1
control of under emergency rule . . 4
defined as enemy 31
duty to check government 5
excluded as enemies in
Trading with Enemy Act 30, 171
fear of government 1
federal class of created 131
included as enemies, amended act 31
made subject to total war powers . 31
money seized by government . . . 31
placed in concentration camps . . 87
treated as enemy 172
Civil Conservation Act 35
civil liberties
in England under emergency rule 118
Civil War
both sides led by moderates . . . 123
did not settle dispute 124
war currency prfits to government 44
south divided into military districts 125
threatened after revolutionary war 168
Civil Work Administration 71
Clinton, President Bill
bombing of Iraq 96
new leadership campaign . . . 164
personal notes on 164
code compliance
as prerequisite for govt business . 52
code making provisions
of NIRA struck down, Supreme Ct 59
Codes of Federal Regulations . . . 66
coin money
congress' loss of power to 37
Congress' power to 22
Cold War 94
beginning of 141
end of 146
collective bargaining
and NIRA 54
required by government stipulation 49
See also trade association codes
colonists
representative bodies dissolved . 13
color and right to vote 19
commerce
control of in Bank Conservation Act 30
records required, Bank Cons. Act 31
US, included as activities of enemy 31
commodities
seizure of under emergency rule . . 4
Commodity Credit Corporation
authorization to make loans . . . 71
formed by executive order 69
stock held by United States 70
commodity prices
deflated to provide cheap food . 107
common law
and right to trial by jury 18
communication
control of in emergency rule . . . 25
control of under emergency rule . . 4
Communism
in Southeast Asia 147, 152
perceived threat of 142
control of North Korea 142
rise to power in Germany 115

competition
  concerns over decline of 88
compliance
  enforced with economic sanctions 75
concentration camps
  US citizens in US camps 93
Confederate States of America
  formation of 123
congress
  delegation of its powers 135
  efforts to end Vietnamese war . . 151
  loss of power during emergency rule 4
  moral responsibilities of members 178
  not in session as civil war began 126
  not informed of aid to allies 90
  power to call up militia 126
  power to coin money 165
  power to coin money usurped . . . 25
  power to declare war 22
  suspend writ of habeas corpus . 127
  OKs Lincoln war powers after fact 128
  refuses Ford's request for Vietnam 151
  taking up abdicated duties 178
  tries to outdo Lincoln in war acts 128
congressional hearings
  on Emergency Banking Act 32
congressional oversight
  Wilson's war powers 135
congressional powers
  usurped by Roosevelt 82
congressional record
  March 9, 1933 . . . . 32, 33, 35, 173
consent of governed 13, 16
constitution
  as barrier to progress 56
  as evolutionary document 66
  as interpreted by Truman 95
  can not be used in court as defense 23
  ignorance of 4
  on powers reserved for people . . 15
  purpose of 16
  suspended during emergency . . 166
  suspended for over 60 years . . . 23
  suspended in Germany 114
constitutional barriers
  to National Recovery Administration 56
Constitutional Development
  book by Carl Brent Swisher . . . 169
constitutional dictatorship . 1, 111, 137
  established in 1933 31
  loss of rights under 2
constitutional rights
  and revolutionary war 4
  suspension of 2
constitutional rule, return to 178
constitutionality
  remarks by Lincoln 125
Consumers Advisory Board 50
containment policy 142
  expanded to include aggression . 144
Continental Dollar 167
contracts
  abrogation of gold clause in . 25, 36
contractual certificates
  in form of Federal Reserve notes 28
contras
  congressional ban on aid to . . . 159
  covert aid given to 158
  money given to under Reagan . . 160
  Reagan claims no knowledge . . 160
control
  during Wilson's term 135
  exercised during WWI 171
  of farm prices 100, 101
  of goods and services 93
  of necessaries under Wilson . . . 136
  over everyday lives 177
controls
  lack of, on Federal Reserve Board 177
Coolidge, President Calvin 137
  optimistic address in 1928 137
  personal notes on 139
Cost of Living Council
  mandatory controls of food prices 99
cotton
  export controls on 104
  importance of before civil war . . 119
  marketing quota 97
  number of slaves working 119
  profits made in North 120
cotton gin
  encourages slavery 119
cotton, short staple
  gains market with cotton gin . . . 119
Council of National Defense 90
court procedure
  regulated by Supreme Court . . . 78
court stacking by Roosevelt 65

credit
as backing for new money system 32
used to back Fed Res bank notes 174
credit expansion
power given to president 37
crimes
as inherently wrong 8
because someone has made a law 8
citizens held guilty of without trial . 21
defined by who is in power 8
criminal sentences
and interstate commerce clause . 75
Cuban Missile Crisis 146
currency
devaluation of 33
need for support of value 38
paper 167
power over as political tool . 137, 177
currency, circulating
not enough to pay national debt . . 175
Czechosolovakia
German invasion of 89

D

Daladier cabinet in France 116
Daniel (Biblical)
and malum prohibitum 8
Davis, Jefferson
as head of Confederate States . 123
assumes emergency power . . . 125
finances fighting with war money 169
personal notes on 124
debt
algebraic equation of 173, 174
as backing for currency 25
as only means to obtain money . 46
by definition, can never be repaid 175
exponential growth of 175
public and private, 1993 43
used to back money system . . . 174
who owes it 175
debt system
representing bondage of people 174
debtor nation, US becomes 158
defense
preparations for WWII 89
defense cuts
requested by Clinton 164
defense spending
of Ronald Reagan 157, 158
deficit
in 1934 43
in 1993 43
deflation
in depression 40
Department of Agriculture 88
See also
Agricultural Adjustment Administration
Agricultural Adjustment Act 39
role in food supply, prices 99
depression
lifestyles during 26
of 1982 157
worldwide in 1930s 113
Desert Shield 162
Desert Storm 159, 162
dictatorial government, Hitler 89
dictatorship
charges leveled at Roosevelt . . . 84
legislative 133
See also constitutional dictatorship
dictatorship in Germany
allowed by Article 48 114
dictatorship laws 83
disparity
in agricultural buying power 38
dollar devaluation
devaluation of in 1933 28
profit goes to government . . . 44, 72
domino theory
reason for Vietnam intervention . 147
proven false in Southeast Asia . 152
Douglas, Stephen A.
claims of states rights on slavery 121
draft
falls on poor in Vietnam war . . 148
Dred Scott decision 65, 121
drought relief 77
drug raids 21
dual citizenship 16
due process
guaranteed by Constitution 17
lack of, in imprisoning Japanese . 93
violation in Bituminous Coal Act . 62
court decision, RR Retirement Act 59
for federal citizens 132
Dutch Guiana
US aid to during neutrality 91

E

Eastern Europe
  Soviet occupation of 141
economic problems
  under Bush 163
  under Reagan 158
  under Clinton 164
economic control after New Deal . . 87
economic crisis in Germany
  dealt with by emergency powers 114
economic dictatorship in Germany 114
economic plan of Ronald Reagan . 157
economic planning experiment . . . 39
economic power concentration
  and National Recovery Act 88
economy
  controlled by Woodrow Wilson . 136
  Effect of Vietnam war on 152
  placed in overdrive during war . 167
  sluggish under Eisenhower . . . 145
Economy Act 35
Eisenhower, President Dwight D.
  opposed expansion of govt powers 144
  personal notes on 145
  SE Asia Treaty Organization . . 144
  treaty with Taiwan 144
  U2 spy plane incident 145
  warning in farewell address . . . 141
El Salvador, US aid to 158
electronic snooping 21
Ellsburg, Daniel
  Nixon burglarized doctor's office 153
  releases study on Vietnam war . 153
embargo, grain 156
emergency 1
  as declared by Fed Reserve Board 37
  declared before WWII 89
  declared in great depression . . . 25
  requiring credit expansion 37
  incentive for 177
emergency banking act . . . 27, 30, 35
  as seiaure act of war 45
  authorizes money based on debt . 32
  See also Bank Conservation Act
Emergency Banking Relief Act . . 175
emergency clause
  in France, Germany, England . . 113
emergency currency 32
  algebraic definition of . . . 173, 174
  based on debt 32
emergency government
  funded through deficit spending . 42
emergency governments
  two operating during civil war . . 130
emergency management
  agencies during WWII 90
emergency powers
  abuse of by government 23
  and Agricultural Adj Administration 38
  as interpreted by FDR 26
  assumed by Abraham Lincoln . . 125
  assumed by Jefferson Davis . . . 125
  during rebellion or invasion 1, 3
  enabling act during depression . . 27
  failure of presidents to end 3
  in France 116
  in Great Britain 117
  in recent times 141
  termination left to president . . 3, 47
  termination of, in name only . . . 110
  used by FDR in depression . . . 25
  See also war powers
emergency powers clause
  Germany's Article 48 3
  in constitution 1
Emergency Powers Continuation Act 94
Emergency Price Control Act . . . 93
Emergency Relief Act 35
Emergency Relief & Construction Act 70
emergency rule
  becomes permanent control . . . 80
  codified into law 175
  ends automatically in England . . 118
  for over 60 years 2, 3, 177
  proclaimed during depression . . 27
emergency war script 173, 174
  Federal Reserve bank notes . . . 32
emergency, economic
  addressed in Ag Adjustment Act . 38
eminent domain
  in public works projects 69
enabling acts
  in France, Germany 114, 116
enemy
  defined as American people . 25, 30
  in Trading with Enemy Act . . 29, 171
enforcement powers
  given to Secretary of Interior . . . 67

equality
  in Declaration of Independence . . 12
Europe
  partitioning of after WWII 94
  rebuilding to fend off Communism 142
evolutionary document
  theory of constitution 66
Ex Parte Merryman 127
ex post facto law
  prohibited by Constitution 23
executive branch
  unchecked by judicial and legislative 3
Executive Order
  establishing Ofc of Emergency Mgmt 90
Executive Order 11533 97
Executive Order 11677 97
Executive Order 2093 79
Executive Order 6199 66
Executive Order 6204 67
Executive Order 6209 68
Executive Order 6225 68
Executive Order 6246 52
Executive Order 6252 68
Executive Order 6340 69
Executive Order 6420 71
Executive Order 6474 71
Executive Order 6581 73
Executive Order 6646 75
Executive Order 6766 78
Executive Order 6777 78
Executive Order 6814 79
Executive Order 7037 79
Executive Order 7065 79
Executive Order 7066
  imprisoning 70,000 US citizens . . 93
Executive Order 8389
  protecting assets of allies 92
Executive Order 8868 91
Executive Order 8928 91
executive orders 22
  between 1933 and 1936 80
  in Germany 114
executive privilege
  Reagan withholding diaries . . . 160
Export Administration Act of 1969 . . 97
export controls
  congressional debate on 98
  on cotton 104
  Senate hearing on . 99, 101, 102, 103
  under guise of national security . . 97
export marketing certificates
  as substitute for export tax 104
export tax
  Senate discussion of 104
Export Import Bank 73
extortion
  interstate commerce clause 76
Ezekial, Mordecai
  on experiment in economic planning 39

F

factories, US, seized by US soldiers
  Air Associates Inc. 91
  Federal Shipbuilding & Drydock Co 91
  North American Aviation plant . . 90
fair competition
  formulated by trade associations . 48
family farmers
  doomed for extinction 107
Farm Credit Act 40, 70
farm market, manipulation of . . . 105
farm prices
  congress OKs lowering of 98
  control of 97, 98
farmers
  in depression in 80s 157
  status of serfdom 46
  subjected to seizure acts of war . 107
farming
  ruled local in character 63
Federal Alcohol Control Admin . . . 71
federal citizens
  created by 14th Amendment . . 132
Federal Communications Commsn . 74
federal deficit in 1982 157
Federal Deposit Insurance Corporation
  and bank robberies 76
  establishment of 36
  guarantees as obligations of people 43
Federal Emergency Relief Act . . . 70
Federal Emergency Relief Administration
  purchases land, destroys cattle . . 78
Federal Farm Loan Act 70
Federal Government
  given police power over states . 132
  role of, conflict between N and S 120
Federal Housing Administration . . 75
federal kidnapping statute 76
Federal Power Commission 74

Federal Radio Commission
  becomes FCC 74
Federal Register
  as vehicle for decrees 22
Federal Reserve
  coining money 22
  formed to finance WWI 170
  tight money under Reagan . . . 157
Federal Reserve Act
  passed in 1913 28
  to secure deposits of gold 28
Federal Reserve bank notes 172, 173
  arbitrary inflation of land value . 107
  as emergency war script 32
  created by debt 40
  debt as security for 34
  not backed by gold 32
  use of arbitrarily propped up value 39
Federal Reserve Banks 72
Federal Reserve Board
  immune from controls 177
  power to adjust reserve balances . 38
  power to declare emergency . . . 37
  gets list of people withdrawing gold 27
Federal Reserve note 32, 173
  as contractual certificate for gold . 29
  as result of war power 177
  backed by gold when established . 28
  holdings, in Emergency Banking Bill 34
  manipulated after WWI 171
  not backed by gold or silver 23
Federal Reserve system
  as debtors to American people . 175
  business restrictions on banks . 109
Federal Shipbuilding & Drydock Co . 91
federal treasury
  confiscated southern property . . 130
Federalist Papers
  definition of tyranny 56
Federalist party 168
federation formed by colonists . . . 15
Fifteenth Amendment 19
Fifth Amendment 129
  in Railroad Retirement Act 59
finance
  dictatorship over, cong. record . . 34
financial transactions of enemies . 171

financing
  control of private in emergency 25, 36
firearms
  carried by Justice Dept. agents . 77
Fireside Chat 86
  hints of income tax 53
First Decontrol Act of 1947 94
Florida secedes from union 123
Food Administration 136
food aid to Somalia 163
Food Stamp Act 105
Ford, President Gerald
  asks for aid to South Vietnam . . . 151
  feud with congress 155
  grain embargo 107
  pardons Nixon 154
  personal notes on 155
  served without election 155
foreign countries
  agreements without congress . . . 89
foreign policy
  furthered with export controls . . . 97
Fort Sumpter
  beginning of Civil War fighting . . . 123
France
  Daladier cabinet in 116
  emergency powers well defined . . 116
  Petain government in 117
freedom
  abridgement of under emergency rule 3
freedom of press 81
  suspended by Lincoln 129
  under constitution 84
French
  financing of colonies in war 168
Fuel Administration 136
fuel alcohol 156

G

Garfield, Harry A. 136
general welfare clause
  limited by specific grants 61
general welfare clause of Constitution
  in Supreme Court case 61
Georgia secedes from union 123
German army in Europe 87
Germany
  emergency clause 113
  partitioning of after WWII 94
Glass Steagall Act
  guaranteeing bank deposits . . . 36

gold
as backing Federal Reserve notes 28
as legal tender 23
as peacetime money 31
authority to impound by Treasury 34
call in as seizure act of war . . . 45
devaluation profits taken by govt 44
fines for withdrawing 29
list of withdrawers published . . . 27
regulation,Trading with Enemy Act 30
run on banks to withdraw 26
seizure of 25, 27, 35, 44
where did it go 43
withdrawals claimed for hoarding 28
gold certificates 72
gold clause
abrogation of in contracts 25, 36, 80
Gold Clause Cases 58
gold dollar
weight reduced by 40% 71
gold policy
squeaks by Supreme Court . . . 58
gold reserve and inflation 33
Gold Reserve Act 71
gold standard
abandonment of 35
Gone with the Wind 132
Gore, Al 164
government
Anti Federalists fear of strong . . 15
as debtors to American people . 175
as enemy of people 31
as tyrant 2
citizenns duty to steer 178
two operating in 1934 42
borrowing requirements in 1934 . 42
control of country during war . . . 166
government news service 83
government spending
in excess of income 41
government's actions
no recourse against 9
government's right to
invade our privacy 9
jail us 9
kill us 9
rob out time and productivity 9
ruin our reputation 9
take our children 9
take our money and property . . . 9
government run magazine 85
grain embargoes 107, 155
Grand Jury
indictment required 17
right to indictment by suspended 129
grazing on public lands 78
Great Britain
economic conditions in 1930s . . 117
emergency powers of Churchill . 117
Great Depression 171
Greenland
US aid to during neutrality 91
Grenada, US invasion of 159
guarantee of deposits
as obligations of people 43
Guatemala
CIA plots concerning 144
guilty until proven innocent 21
Gulf of Sidra 159
Gulf War Syndrome 163

H

habeas corpus, writ of 22
suspended by Lincoln 127
Haiti, US occupation of 164
Harpers Ferry
arsenal seized by John Brown . 122
Hathaway, Senator
on administered prices . . . 102, 103
health insurance 158
Hindenburg, Paul von 114
Hiroshima 87, 94
Hiss, Alger 142
Hitler, Adolf
dictator through emergency power 113
dictatorial government 3, 89
publicity department of 85
scrapping of Weimar Constitution 116
hoarding
included as act of enemy 30
Home Owners Loan Act 36, 40
to prop up values, bail out banks . 39
homelessness
added to nation's vocabulary . . 158
homes
government control of financing 25, 36
homestead act desired by north . 122
Hoover, President Herbert
as head of Food Administration . 136

claim that gold missing from vaults 28
personal notes on 139
problems after inauguration . . . 138
refuses to act on bankers resolution 28
Hoovervilles 26
hot oil case 63, 68
House of Commons
airs issues under emergency rule 117
housing during great depression . . 26
Hundred Days, The 35
Hungarian Revolution
Eisenhower doesn't send troops 144
Hussein, Saddam 162

I

immigrant labor, industrial revolution 120
immunity, government
against prosecution 80
import quotas on sugar 106
imports
north and south conflict over . . 120
duty exempt livestock feed 79
income tax
hinted at in second Fireside Chat . 53
passed to cover war money . . . 170
retroactive as ex post facto law . . 23
Independence, Declaration of 12
indictment
by Grand Jury required 17
by Grand Jury, suspended in war . 17
individual responsibility 178
Indonesia
CIA plots concerning 144
Industrial Advisory Board 50
industrial regions
in depression in 80s 157
industry
bound by trade association codes . 48
control by Codes of Federal Regs . 66
control of under Wilson 136
deregulation of under Reagan . . 157
gov't control of in emergency . . . 25
nationalization of 3, 47
inflation
and export controls 97
and gold standard 33
and deficit financing, Vietnam war 150
export controls to curb 98
to meet government obligations . . 33
international law
attack on Pearl Harbor 92
Roosevelt charged with breaking . 90
violation of during neutrality 87, 90, 91
international police force 94
interstate commerce
and pension funds 59
control by pres. unconstitutional . 57
does not include coal mining . . . 62
in Supreme Court decision 60
interstate commerce clause
and bank robberies 76
and racketeering 77
and stolen goods 76
in felonies and witness testimony 76
used to control criminal sentences 76
Interstate Commerce Commission . 74
interstate communications
and extortion 76
intrastate commerce
not within government's power . 62
invasions
and emergency powers 1
of Kuwait 162
of Panama 162
US invasion of Grenada 159
Iran
arms sold to by Reagan admin . . 160
CIA plots concerning 144
hostages taken by 155
hostages, attempt to rescue . . . 156
Iraq war 95
congress' support not necessary . 96
no resolution to 162
under auspices of UN 96
1994 crisis 164
Iron Curtain 94, 142
term coined by Churchill 118
Israel 164

J

Japan
bombing of 94
colonization of Manchuria, Korea 89
threat to China 89
Japanese
imprisoned during WWII . . . 87, 93
Jay, John
agrees to pay war reparations . . 168

Jefferson, President Thomas . . . 168
and Declaration of Independence 12
jeopardy, double 17, 21
Johnson, General
and National Recovery Admin . . 53
Johnson, President Andrew
reconstruction plan 131
Johnson, President Lyndon B. . . . 146
escalation of Vietnam War 147
personal notes on 149
judicial system
examiing entrenched war powers 178

K

Kansas
as battleground over slavery . . . 121
Kansas Nebraska Act 121
Kennedy, President John F.
assasination of 146
idealism and nationalism under . 145
introduces reform legislation . . . 146
personal notes on 146
Kent State University 150
King George
attitude toward colonists 11
complaints against 13
knowledge as power 4
Korean War 89
as police action 94
concluded by Eisenhower 144
death toll from 143
ended in stalemate 143
north invasion of south 143
partitioning of after police action . 94
Truman as leader in 143
under auspices of UN 96
US economic aid to 143
Kruschev, Nikita 144
Kurds 163
Kuwait 163

L

labor
govt control of in emergency . . . 25
immigrant and slave, pre civil war 120
nationalization of 36
wage and hour mandates 48
Labor Advisory Board 50
labor disputes
Montgomery Ward 87
land
acquisition by government 80
prices arbitrarily inflated 107
purchased by government 78
land use 79
regulated by Natl Resources Board 78
Laos, CIA plots concerning 144
law enforcement
agreements among states 77
lawsuit
forbidden against government . . 81
League of Nations
Wilson's involvement in 137
Lebanon
US troops sent to 144, 159
legislative crisis government
congress takes reins after civil war 132
legislative powers
vested in congress 22
Lend Lease Act
giving foreign nations war materials 92
Lever Act
allowed control of necessaries . 136
liberties
sold back in form of license 8
liberty
as purpose of Constitution 16
restriction of does not buy safety . . 9
Roosevelt on 56
Libya, US bombing of 159
licenses
in amended Trading w Enemy Act 30
licensing
and anti trust laws 48
required in all industry 66
under Woodrow Wilson 136
limited emergency
declared by Roosevelt 89
Senate Report 93-549 90
Lincoln Dictatorship 127
Lincoln, Abraham
as moderate candidate 122
assumes emergency power . . . 125
finances fighting with war money 169
race against Stephen A. Douglas 121
raises armies, against law . . . 126
Louisiana secedes from union . . 123
loyalty oath
required of southerners 132

M

MacArthur, General Douglas
  commander in chief, Korean War 143
  leads troops against US veterans 138
mail, opening of by CIA 156
malum prohibitum
  crime against a law 8
malum se
  evil in itself 8
management by crisis 177
management by planning 177
Manchuria 89
manufacturing
  ruled local in character 63
marketing quotas 106
Marshall Plan 94, 142
martial law
  definition of 125
  imprisoning US citizens, Japanese 93
  imposed on south after war 125, 129
  president's power to institute . . . 25
Mayaguez, US Freighter 155
McCarthy, Joseph R.
  claims communist conspiracy . 142
McDonald, Ramsay 117
McFadden, Congressman 173
  on dictatorship over finance 34
McGugin, Representative
  on gold standard, in cong. record . 33
meat production 101
Medicare 146
military
  superior to civil power in colonies . 13
military districts
  southern states as 169
military forces under emergency rule
  pres. power to send abroad . . 4, 25
militia, state
  Lincoln calls, against constitution 126
Milligan case 129
mind control experiments
  carried out by CIA 156
minds
  control of 177
minimum wage law
  declared unconstitutional 63
mining, ruled local in character . . . 63
Missouri Compromise 121
Mitchell, Margaret 132
money
  equation of war currency . . 173, 174
  and Federal Reserve 22
  backed by debt 32
  colonists lack of coins for trade . . 11
  congress' power to regulate . . . 27
  control of 177
  created by government obligations 40
  created by private mortgages . . 40
  devaluation of, and gold reserve . 33
  devalued by reducing gold content 71
  emergency currency 31
  lack of money system in colonies 11
  method of borrowing into existence 46
  minted in colonies 12
  power to coin 165
  power to coin given to pres . . 37, 47
  power to coin, in Ag Adjustment Act 25
  printing to pay depositors 34
  printing, to meet govt expenses . 33
  required during war 167
  seized by government orders . . 31
  war money and peace money . . 165
  value of propped up 38
money system
  creation of modern day 39
money, peace
  represents prosperity 165
money, war, represents debt 165
monopolies
  Roosevelt's view of 88
Montgomery Ward
  assets seized during war . . . 87, 93
moon, man on
  challenge by Kennedy 145
moral high road 178
Morehead v New York ex red Tipaldo 63
mortgage
  as backing for new money system 32
  as only means to acquire money . 46
  as basis for new money system . 32
mortgages, defaulted
  turned to govt guaranteed bonds . 39
most favored nation principle . . . 79
My Lai massacre
  committed by US troops 149

N

Nagasaki 87, 94
national budget in 1934 41

national crisis
  spurred by Joseph McCarthy . . 142
national debt, cost of servicing . . 158
Natl Emergency Termination Act . 110
Natl Housing Act 75
Natl Industrial Recvry Act 36, 54, 70, 73
  attempt to redistribute population . 68
  declared unconstitutional 57
  delegation of powers 68
  nationalizing industry 47
  concentrating economic power . . 88
  See also
    NIRA, Nat'l Recovery Admin
National Recovery Administration
  as permanent government function 54
  reorganization of 53
national resource use 79
  regulated by Natl Resource Board 78
National Resources Committee . . . 80
  duties of 79
nationalization
  based on Trading with Enemy Act . 37
  of agriculture 36
  of America 37
  of contracts 36
  of currency and commerce 35
  of home financing 36
  of industry 36
  of labor 36
  of labor and industry 66
  of natural resources 35
  of private financing 36
  of social agenda 35
  of transportation 36
  of utilities 36
natural resources
  govt control of in emergency . . . 25
Navy patrols of Canadian coasts
  during neutrality 91
Nazis, rise to power in Germany . 115
Nebraska
  as battleground over slavery . . 121
necessary measures
  defined in Germany 114
Netherlands
  US aid to during neutrality 91
neutrality
  aid to allies during 91
  claimed by US 89
  escorting arms to Britain during . . 92
neutrality patrols 92
New Deal
  as windfall to moneychangers . . 28
  merged into war regime 88
  publicized by White House Press . 86
New Jewel Movement in Grenada 159
new money
  based on obligations of people . . 43
  to finance emergency government 43
  without creating debt 166
Nicaragua 159, 160
Nineteenth Amendment 19
Nixon, President Richard M.
  and export controls 98
  attitude toward law violation . . 153
  attitude toward war powers . . . 150
  bombing of Cambodia 149
  burglary regarding Daniel Ellsburg 153
  personal notes on 154
  price freezes and grain embargo 107
  re escalates Vietnam war 149
  resigns due to Watergate scandal 153
  resists efforts to end Vietnam war 151
  wage and price freeze under . . 154
  Watergate scandal 151
nobility, titles of 172
Noriega, Manuel 162
north
  industrial economy of 120
North American Aviation Plant
  seized by US soldiers 90
North, Oliver 160
  conviction overturned 161
  indictment and convistion of . . 160
  role in Grenada invasion 159
  testimony of 160
nuclear missiles
  US deployment in Europe . . . 159

O

oath, loyalty 132
  imposed on southerners 130
Office of Emergency Management . 90
Office of War Mobilization 90
Olympics, US boycott of 156
opposition
  to Roosevelt's programs 81
organization of industry
  to prevent overproduction 48

original understanding doctrine
  theory of constitution 66
ownership of property
  only by virtue of government . . . 36

P

Panama Canal
  defense of during WWII 91
  return of to Panama 156
Panama Refining Co. vs Bran . . . 57
Panic of 1857 122
parity
  of currency, regulated by president 37
Patman, Representative 174
  on Emergency Banking Bill 33
  on new money system 32
peace agreements
  Israel and PLO 164
Peace Corps 145, 146
peace money 165
  limited use of 165
Peace Movement
  infiltrated by CIA 148
peace, world
  as responsibility of US 142
peacetime money 31, 111
  never returned to people 172
  seizure by government 172
Pearl Harbor 87
  and international law 92
Pentagon Papers
  Vietnam misrepresented 152
Petain government in France . . . 117
petroleum
  regulation in interstate commerce . 66
petroleum industry
  regulated by NIRA 57
PLO 164
plots formulated by CIA 144
Poindexter, John M. 160, 161
Poland, German threat to 89
police power
  federal government over states . 132
political party
  president as head of 96
politicians as servants of citizens . 178
poll taxes and 24th Amendment . . 19
poor
  number of increase under Reagan 158
population
  redistribution of through NIRA . . 68
powers
  reserved for people 15, 18
president
  as head of political party 96
  control over Federal Reserve . . 110
  given power over money system . 37
  invasions of foreign countries . . 22
  powers under emergency rule . . . 4
president's authority
  to set export controls 103
President's Reemployment Agreement
  enforced by ostracism, sanctions 52
presidential proclamations
  between 1933 and 1936 80
  See also Executive Orders, Proclamations
press
  government control of credit for . 85
press censorship 83
price ceilings
  on agricultural products 105
price fixing agreements
  allowed under NIRA 48
price freezes 107
price of wheat
  same as 90 years ago 107
price fixing
  of coal 62
  under Wilson 136
Prisoners of War in Vietnam 150
privacy, invasion of 21
private enterprise
  control of in emergency rule . . 4, 25
private power 88
private property
  not to be taken for public use . . 17
Proclamation 2038 issued by FDR . 26
Proclamation 2039 . . . . . . 172, 175
  claims unwarranted gold w'drawal . 28
  contains resolution by bankers . . 28
  proclaims bank holiday 27
  stops withdrawals of gold 27
Proclamation 2040
  based on act not yet passed . . . 29
  based on Trading with Enemy Act 29
  continues Proclamation 2039 . . 27
Proclamation 2072 71
Proclamation 2914 97

Proclamation 4074 97
Proclamation 5071 106
Proclamation 5294 106
proclamations by president 22
production
  control of in emergency rule . . 4, 25
  curtailment of, to prop up prices . . 39
property
  confiscated in south 130
  confiscation of 21
  ownership by virtue of govt 25
  mortgages on, as assets of banks . 32
  ownership as mere users 36
  ownership is in state 36
  power to seize in emergency rule . 25
  requisitioned for war effort 91
  seized in south 131
  seizure of 2, 4
  use subordinate to state 25
prosperity, false
  based on debt 43
protests
  against Vietnam war 148
Proxmire, Senator
  on export controls 100
public debt
  in 1934 . . . . 42, 43
  in 1993 43
public information
  controlled by Lincoln 129
public lands 78
  use of decreed by government . . 78
public opinion
  as enforcer of trade codes 50
Public Papers of Herbert Hoover . . 28

Public Papers, Roosevelt
  and census bureau 68
  and drought relief 78
  and population redistribution . . . 68
  Blue Eagle to denote compliance . 52
  disallowing suits against govt . . . 81
  govt gets profits from war currency 45
  grazing on public lands 78
  licensing and anti trust laws 48
  NY minimum wage law 63
  on Commodity Credit Corporation . 71
  on enforcing compliance 75
  on Export Import Bank 74
  on FCC 74
  on Federal Housing Administration 75
  on industrial recovery 51
  on wage, price controls 51
  on liberty and constitution 56
  on national resource regulation . . 79
  on nationalizing silver 45
  on public works 69
  on reducing gold content of dollar 72
  on regulating criminal sentences . 77
  on rulings of unconstitutionality 57, 63
  on trade with other countries . . . 75
  on trade assocs and anti trust laws 49
  on where the gold went 43
  petroleum regulation 67
  rebuttal of unconstitutional rulings 65
  Senator Schall's opposition . . . 86
  speech at Vassar College 53
  Supreme Court and lower courts . 78
public relations
  Roosevelt's concern with 89
public safety and order
  endangered in Germany 114
public works 36, 67, 69
  financing of railroad maintenance . 69
  under Federal Emergency Admin . 69
Public Works Administration
  established by executive order . . 68
publicity departments
  of Mussolini 85
  of Hitler run by Goebbels 85
  of Washington Administration . . . 85
  Soviet Tass Agency 85
punishment
  cruel and unusual, Waco, Texas . . 22
  right against cruel or unusual . . . 18
  without trial or conviction 22

R

race and right to vote 19
racketeering
  and interstate commerce clause . 77
Railroad Coordination Act 36
railroad maintenance
  financed as public works project . 69
Railroad Retirement Act
  ruled unconstitutional 59
Railroad Retirement Bd v Alton RR 59
railroads, control of under Wilson . 136
Rayburn Communications Act . . . 84

Reagan, President Ronald
  declares economy in crisis . . . 157
  grain embargo under 107
  personal notes on 161
  testimony on Iran Contra affair . 161
Reciprocal Trade Agreement 75
reclaiming our country
  right and duty to 178
reconstruction of Kuwait 163
reconstruction amendments 133
Reconstruction Finance Corp Act 70, 73
reconstruction of south
  congress overrides Johnson . . 131
recourse
  against government's power . . . 9
reform legislation
  introduced by Kennedy 146
regulation of currency
  power given to president 37
Reichstag in pre war Germany . . 115
representation denied to colonists . 13
republic
  new, formed by colonists 16
revolt
  president can claim war powers . 128
revolution in attitudes 4
Revolutionary War 4
Rhee, Synghman 143
rights
  against double jeopardy 17
  against private property 17
  against unlawful search, seizure . 17
  constitutional vs. reality 16
  Declaration of, 1774 11
  speech, religion, press 16, 17
  government role in 13
  implied, of gov't to protect agencies 76
  inalienable (unalienable) . . . 13, 16
  no warrant without probable cause 17
  not to witness against self 17
  of people to institute new govt . . . 13
  reserved for people 16, 18
  to bear arms 17, 21
  to bear arms, abridgement of . . . 23
  to life, liberty, pursuit of happiness 13
  to no excessive bail or punishment 18
  to speedy trial 18
  to trial by jury 18
  to vote and 15th Amendment . . . 19
roaring twenties 171
Rockefeller, Nelson 156
Roosevelt Papers
  on budget in 1934 42
Roosevelt, President Franklin D.
  and emergency powers 1
  as Assistant Secretary of Navy . . 136
  assumes war powers 172
  criticism of before WWII 90
  death of 86, 87
  declares "limited emergency" . . 89
  defends policies 55
  inaugural address 26
  on returning powers to people . . 87
  opinion on private power 87
  personal facts 86
  response to economic depression 25
  seizure of US factories 90
Rossiter, Clinton
  comments on Lincoln's acts . . . 126
rule
  by statute or decree 1
  without constitutional process . . . 4
rural America in depression in 80s . 157
Rural Electrification Administration . 79
Russia, aid to requested 164

S

Saar region, German threat to . . . 89
safety
  not bought by curtailed liberties . . 9
Sandanistas
  CIA attempt to overthrow 159
Schall, Senator Thomas D.
  opposition to Roosevelt . . . 81, 86
Schechters Poultry Corp. v US . 60, 64
Schlesinger, Arthur
  interpretation of Ag Adjustment Act 39
Schwarzkopf, General Norman
  led Grenada invasion 159
script as emergency currency . . . 32
search and seizure 21
  rights against unlawful 17
SEATO 144, 147
secession from union
  South Carolina leads 122
Second Decontrol Act of 1947 . . . 94
Secord, Major General Richard . . 160
Secretary of War
  authority of under Wilson 137
Securities Act of 1933 40

Securities Exchange Commission . 40
security
for Federal Reserve bank notes . 174
seizure
of peacetime money 172
of rebels' property 129
of US property during WWII . . . 87
under Trading with Enemy Act . . 30
seizure actions of war
grain embargoes, price freezes . 107
seizure of US factories by US soldiers
Air Associates Incorporated . . . 91
Federal Shipbuilding & Drydock Co 91
North American Aviation plant . . 90
selective service and lottery system 149
Senate poll on ending war powers . 108
Senate Document No. 43 36
Senate Hearing, export controls . . 99
Senate Report 93-549 . . . . 1, 3, 175
on limited emergency 90
Shay's Rebellion 168
Sherman Anti Trust Act
See anti trust laws
Shiite 163
silver
as legal tender 23
as peacetime money 31
called in by executive order . . . 79
nationalized in 1934 . . . . . 45, 46
seizure of during depression . . . 25
slanted data
published by government 85
slavery
abolished by Article 13 19
boosted by invention of cotton gin 119
boundaries, free and slave states 121
batleground in Kansas, Nebraska 121
no viable plans to eliminate . . . 120
radical voices heard 119
right to strike assumed by govt . 131
Supreme Court: can't be outlawed 121
thought dying out 119
slaves
brought by Northern ships 120
no rights to sue; not citizens . . . 121
numbers before civil war 119
social agenda
govt control of in emergency . . . 25
social aid
cutback under Reagan 157
Social Democrats in Germany
loss of power 115
soldier's bonus
demanded by veterans 138
soldiers
quartering of in war and peacetime 17
Somalia
troops committed without congress 96
under auspices of UN 96
US troops sent to 163
south
agricultural economy of 120
as prize of war 169
divided into military districts . . 125
economy before civil war 119
economic damage lingers . . . 170
required to pay costs of war . . 170
threatened by Harpers Ferry raid 122
South Carolina
secedes from union 122
Soviet Union, aid to requested . . 164
special interest groups
outgrowth of trade associations . . 48
speculation
during 1920s 171
in Continental Dollars 167
stock market, in 1929 138
spy rings in US 142
stabilization of currency
power given to president 37
Stalin 141
standard of living
business' responsibility to provide 88
state ownership of all property . . . 36
state of siege in France
only declared by a law 116
states
no legal states in south after war 132
states rights
thought superior to federal laws 120
feud becomes civil war 119
reversal of federal and state roles 133
versus federal supremacy 15
Steagall, Congressman 173
on Federal Reserve Bank notes . 34
Stevenson, Sen. on export controls 100
stock market
collapse in 1987 161
crash in 1929 . . . . 26, 138

stolen goods
  interstate commerce clause 76
Stone, Justice
  opinion on Gold Clause Cases . . 58
Strategic Arms Limiitation Treaty . 156
students killed by US troops . . . 150
Suez Canal
  cease fire under Eisenhower . . 144
sugar, import quotas on 106
Sumner, Senator Charles
  caned in senate over slavery . . 122
Supreme Court
  decision on Oliver North 161
  on duties of citizens 5
  orders Nixon to turn over tapes . 154
  regulating lower court procedure . 78
  rules slavery protected 121
Supreme Court justices
  Roosevelt tries to up number of . . 66
Swisher, Carl Brent 169

T

Taney, Chief Justice 127
tariff cuts under John F. Kennedy . 145
tariff rates fixed secretly 83
tax
  income tax to cover war money . 170
  to raise war revenue 168
tax clause
  used to control criminal sentences 76
tax correctives 88
tax cuts
  for wealthy under Reagan . 157, 158
taxation
  to promote national welfare 61
  without representation, in colonies 12
taxes
  levied in south 130
  new taxes requested by Clinton . 164
  to benefit "neighbors" 53
  to meet government expenses . . 33
taxes, direct 22
  levied on southern rebels 129
taxpayers
  obligations to guarantee deposits . 43
teach-ins 148
Temporary Natl Economic Committee 88
Tennessee Valley Authority 36
terrorist attacks blamed on Libya . 159
Tet Offensive 149
Texas secedes from union 123
Third Reich
  and war and emergency powers . 113
Thomas Amendment, Farm Relief Act 71
Title 12 US Code 175
Tonkin Resolution
  free rein to escalate Vietnam war 148
  congress repeals, Nixon ignores . 150
Tonkin Gulf incident
  as excuse for attacking N. Vietnam 147
trade agreements
  See also code compliance
  enforced by ostracism, sanctions 52
trade association agreements
  exempt from anti trust laws 49
trade association codes
  must be approved by president . 48
trade associations
  required by NIRA 48
trade with other countries
  power given to president 75
Trading with Enemy Act 170
  amended by banking act in 1933 . 30
  amended, includes domestic trade 37
  amended, includes US citizens 30, 37
  as basis for emergency powers . 25
  as basis for nationalization 37
  as basis for nationalizing silver . . 46
  as basis for war powers 172
  exclusion of US citizens 30
  regulation of commerce under . . 30
  retained after WWI 136
  text of 29
transportation
  control of in emergency rule . . 4, 25
  nationalization of 36
travel
  restricted under emergency rule 4, 25
treaty
  procedures ignored by Roosevelt 89
trial, right to suspended 129
  speedy 21
trial by jury 21, 23
  right of citizens to 18
trickle down wealth 158
Tripoli 159
Truman Doctrine 142

Truman, President Harry S
- bombing of Japan 87, 94
- personal information on 111
- views of constitution 95

Truth in Securities 36
Twenty Fourth Amendment 19
Twenty Sixth Amendment 19
Two Faces of Debt 175
tyranny defined by Madison 56

U

U2 spy plane 145
unconstitutional acts by congress
- during civil war 129

unconstitutional acts, Lincoln 126. 129
- Lincoln ignores ruling of illegality 127
- govt money to private persons . 127
- suspends writ of habeas corpus . 127

unconstitutional rulings
- abrogation, gold clause in contracts 58
- Agricultural Adjustment Act 60
- Bituminous Coal Conservation Act 62
- code making provisions of NIRA . 59
- labor prov. of Bituminous Coal Act 63
- National Industrial Recovery Act . 57
- NY minimum wage law 63
- plan to increase number of justices 65
- Railroad Retirement Act 59
- rebutted by Roosevelt 64
- stacked court reverses 66

uniform extradition procedure 77
United Nations 94
- as world police force 96

United States
- claims of neutrality in WWII 89

United States Code
- war powers made part of 110

United States v Butler 61
unwarranted delegation of power
- in Bituminous Coal Act 62

US role as world police force 96
US convoys
- escorting arms during neutrality . . 92

US troops
- kill students at Kent State 150
- massacre civilians at My Lai . . . 149
- used against citizens under Wilson 137

USSR
- accused in North Korean invasion 143

utilties
- nationalization of 36
- govt control of in emergency . . . 25

V

Vance
- Secretary of State Cyrus 156

Vassar College
- Roosevelt's speech at 52

veterans, needy
- marching on Washington D.C. . 138

Vietnam 95
- advisors in, under Kennedy . . . 146
- agreement on without South . . 150
- bombing of 148
- credibility gap in 149
- defense tactics to search, destroy 148
- Eisenhower does not send troops 144
- expenses for 148, 152
- Johnson decides to de-escalate 149
- massive bombing under Nixon . 150
- no resolution to conflict 152
- policy leading to 144
- protests against war in 148
- South declares third war, asks aid 151
- surrender of South 152
- under auspices of UN 96
- US promises to rebuild north . . 151
- war escalated under Johnson . 147
- war misrepresented to citizens . 152

voting age lowered to 18 19

W

Waco, Texas
- cruel punishment without trial . . . 22

wage and hour laws
- in Supreme Court case 59

wage and price freeze
- under Nixon 154

wage, hour agreements
- as local concern 63

Walsh, Lawrence 161
war
- beginning of WWII 87
- begins in Europe 89
- control over country during . . . 166
- exercise upon American people . 172
- no longer declared by congress . . 96
- no need for declaration of 94
- president's power to involve in . . . 96

war activities
  without congress' approval 91
war amendments
  during civil war period 133
war and emergency powers
  abuse of 23
war currency
  Continental Dollar 167
  profits from during civil war 44
War Industries Board 136
war materials
  power to give to other countries . . 92
war money 165
  as cause of great depression . . 171
  as debt upon people 167
  as paper currency 167
  as reparation of war 165
  during WWI 170, 171
  finances civil war 169
  manipulated after WWI 171
  raised by taxation 168
war on Iraq, costs of 163
War on Poverty 146
war powers
  agencies' request to broaden . . 108
  assumed by Lincoln 128
  extended after WWII ended 94
  in Emergency Banking Bill 34
  includes control over citizens . . . 31
  placed people in state of bondage . 46
  reaffirmed in 1952 94
  Roosevelt promised back to people 94
  used by Woodrow Wilson 135
  used to aid allies 87, 91
  used to create Ag Adj Admin. . . . 38
  used to imprison 70,000 US citizens 87
  used to seize Montgomery Ward . . 93
  See also emergency powers
War Powers of the Executive in the US
  book by Clarence A. Bordahl . . . 171
war powers termination
  Senate poll on 108
War Powrs Act
  passed over Nixon's veto 151
war reparations
  applied against South 169
  demanded by Hanoi 152
  of revolutionary war 167
war, WWII
  US position of neutrality 87
wars
  not fought to conclusion 94
wartime money 31
  See also emergency currency
wartime taxation
  direct taxes on citizens 129
water use 79
  regulated by Natl Resources Board 78
Watergate 151
weapons
  traded to allies during neutrality . . 90
Weimar Constitution 114
  scrapped by Hitler 116
welfare program 35
welfare system
  government control of 25
wheat marketing quota 97, 106
  price same as 90 years ago 107
White House Press
  official news service of New Deal . 86
Whitney, Eli 119
wildlife conservation
  established by executive order . . 78
Wilson, President Woodrow
  personal notes on 139
  use of war powers 135
wiretapping 21
  restrictions placed on by Carter . . 156
witnesses, extradition of 77
women
  and right to vote, 19th Amendment 19
world police, US role in 96
World War I 136
writ of habeas corpus 22
  suspension of in emergency rule . 22

Y

Yalta Conference 141